ft Fitness Trainers

Running for Fitness

D0260400

Dedication

This book is dedicated to my partner, Grethe Petersen, and to my family. You all bring more joy to my life than I know how to express.

I owe an enormous amount to the members of the Serpentine Running Club: thank you for sharing your experience, and for your support and friendship. Thank you also to Frank Horwill, a running legend, for his knowledge, wisdom and inspiration.

Thank you to Paul Ashworth, Brian Barder, Charlotte Jenkins, Leigh Kenney, David Knight, Phil McCubbins, Grethe Petersen, Rebecca Stubbs, Swenja Surminski and Sonia Wilson for comments on earlier drafts; all remaining errors are, of course, my own.

The author

Published in 2002 by A & C Black Publishers Ltd
37 Soho Square, London W1D 3QZ

Copyright © 2002 by Owen Barder

ISBN 0 7136 5139 3

A CIP catalogue record for this book is available from the British Library.

Note: Whilst every effort has been made to ensure that the content of this book is as technically accurate and as sound as possible, neither the authors nor the publishers can accept responsibility for any injury or loss sustained as a result of the use of this material.

Acknowledgements

All photographs by David Knight except those on pages 7, 14, 26, 89, 95, 109, 115 by Owen Barder.
Line illustrations by Jean Ashley.
Cover image © Jump, Hamburg.
Chapter 6 – Calorie Intake Calculations based on a table in Anita Bean, *The Complete Guide to Sports Nutrition*, A & C Black, 2000. Chapter 7 – Box on 'What to look for in an ideal sports drink' reproduced with permission from Tim Noakes, *The Lore of Running*, Oxford University Press, 2001. Table 9.1 Frank Horwill's Five Tier Training System adapted from Frank Horwill, *An Obsession for Running*, British Milers' Club, 1991. Table 10.3 Training Intensities Based on Current VO_2 max – Reproduced from Jack Daniels, *Daniels' Running Formula*, 1998, Human Kinetics, Champaign Illinois. Tables 11.1 and 11.2 Race Time Comparison and Predictor Charts – Reproduced from Bob Glover and Shelly-lynn Florence Glover, *The Competitive Runner's Handbook*, Penguin Books, 1999.

A & C Black uses paper produced with elemental chlorine-free pulp, harvested from managed sustainable forests.

Typeset in 10/12pt Minion Display

Printed and bound in Great Britain by Biddles Ltd, Guildford and King's Lynn.

Contents

Preface

This is a book about running; but it is also a book about runners. Though I have been around runners for a long time now, they continue to amaze me.

Running has a reputation for being a sport for loners, an image immortalised in Alan Sillitoe's *The Loneliness of the Long Distance Runner*. The runners I know do indeed have quiet determination, a strong sense of self-worth and deep reserves of inner strength. But in my experience, runners are not introverts. They are outgoing, sharing and considerate. Runners seem to have the unusual quality of being equally confident in their own company and in the company of others. To me, this suggests that running can help us to reach an elusive inner balance.

Running is a very honest sport. You get out what you put in. If you haven't done the training for a marathon, you can't fake it. But if you put in the work, you will reap the rewards. There is nothing flash and nothing glamorous about the sport; just honest hard work. Perhaps this helps to explain the straightforward and open character of the runner.

This book is written both for beginners and more experienced runners. There is advice to beginners to get you started, and then help for you to progress further, to develop your health, fitness and running. Although some of the discussion about training techniques in the later chapters won't appear at first to be relevant to a complete beginner, there is plenty of advice that will help to lay the foundations of a long, safe and enjoyable pastime.

Such wisdom as there is in this book is a composite of my own experiences and those of my friends and fellow runners, who have been kind enough to share what they have learned from many years of running. Like so many others, I have also benefited enormously from the great running writers, such as Tim Noakes, George Sheehan, Frank Horwill and Hal Higdon. There is, in Noakes's words, a shared *lore of running* from which this book draws; I hope that, in a small way, it also contributes to that community of knowledge.

If this book helps one person to become physically active, or one experienced runner to avoid an injury, or if one jogger is inspired to be the best that they can be, then it will have made a positive contribution to the world. And that is all we can ask of ourselves.

Owen Barder
London, 2002

Running is not what I do: it is an essential part of who I am. If you ask most people to describe themselves, as likely as not they will tell you what they do for a living. Most of the runners I know don't define themselves by their job. They will tell you something about their life outside work. This chapter is about the many different reasons why we are runners.

The evolution of runners

One of the great sports writers of the twentieth century, Dr George Sheehan, suggested that every runner evolves through three stages:[1]

- first, **joggers** take up exercise to lose weight and get more fit; they are obsessed about their weight; and often evangelise their friends and colleagues about the physical benefits of running;
- then one day the jogger enters a race, and attention shifts. **Racers** concentrate on improving their performance, beating their personal bests and competing. The mental effort of racing improves the mind, just as jogging improves the body;
- and finally, the racer may become a **runner**, who enjoys the physical benefits of running, and continues to value fitness. Runners take part in races, and try to be the best they can, but they no longer expect every race to be a personal best. They run to find peace of mind.

'Jogging, they say, is competing against yourself. Racing is competing against others. Running is discovering that competing is only competing. It is essential and not essential. It is important and unimportant. Running is finally seeing everything in perspective. Running is discovering the wholeness, the unity that everyone seeks. Running is the fusion of body, mind, and soul in that beautiful relaxation that joggers and racers find so difficult to achieve.'

George Sheehan, Running to Win, 1992

Of course, in real life there is something of all of George Sheehan's three stages in every runner. But there is a perceptible progression of most runners through these different phases.

The last stage – the runner – is the most difficult to describe to those who have not experienced it first-hand. Running can bring a kind of inner strength and self-confidence. The effect of this can be witnessed in any gathering of runners – for example, at a running club, or at a local road race. There you will meet a group of people who have an unusual mixture of qualities: they have a sense of self-worth, without being arrogant or self-centred; they are equally comfortable in a large group of people or with their own company; they are willing to face up to challenges; and they have an understanding that, whatever we do in our lives, real satisfaction comes when we know that we have been the best that we can be.

For women, in particular, running can be strongly empowering. Some women feel under enormous pressure from society to conform to unachievable (and unhealthy) standards of physical appearance and weight, which can sometimes lead to eating disorders and depression. Running can liberate women from the tyranny of dieting and eating anxieties, and create a self-esteem that helps them to take control of their lives.

Fitness

Running is to sport as playing the piano is to music. It is an essential building block of many sporting activities, from football to cricket. Even for sports that don't involve running directly – such as skiing or ice hockey – running is often an important part of the athlete's training programme. This is partly because running is cheap, and requires no special skills, equipment or organisation with team-mates. But it is also because running is an especially efficient way to increase fitness. Very few other sports – perhaps only swimming, rowing and cross-country skiing – have such clear benefits in terms of all-round fitness.

What is fitness? How is it different from health?

Health means freedom from illness or injury, enabling a person to live normally and in comfort. *Fitness* means the ability to expend a lot of energy efficiently.

Fitness can be measured in many different dimensions. There are people who can lift huge weights efficiently, but could not comfortably run a mile. Weightlifters can generate huge bursts of energy for a short period of time, using their upper body. By contrast, there are marathon runners who would have the greatest difficulty performing simple gymnastics on parallel bars because they lack upper body strength, but who can propel their body around a 26.2-mile course with great efficiency. Both the weightlifter and the marathon runner are fit, in that they can expend energy efficiently, but they are fit in different ways.

Cardiovascular fitness means the ability of your body to absorb oxygen and transfer it through the blood supply to the muscles. The efficiency of your heart and lungs and health of your arteries are an important determinant of cardiovascular fitness. It is especially important for sports that require energy to be expended over a prolonged period of time, in which the fuel and oxygen needed to generate motion are not all stored in the muscles that do the work.

Fitness tests are generally aimed at measuring your cardiovascular fitness. But the fitness levels observed in a test depend both on your underlying cardiovascular fitness, and on the ability of particular muscle groups to translate energy efficiently in the activity used in the test – for example, your chest muscles to do press-ups, or your legs when you run. This means that a trained runner will generally perform better in a fitness test on a treadmill than in a fitness test on an exercise bike.

How does running make you fit?

All fitness is acquired through a process of physical stress and recovery.

When you exercise, your body is required to do things that it does not normally do when you are resting. For example, when you run, your heart beats faster, your muscles work harder and your metabolic system burns more fuel to transfer energy. When you stop the exercise, your body recovers *and adapts to make it easier to do this in future*. It is important to remember that your body's adaptation occurs when you are recovering, not while you are actually undertaking the effort. This is why rest is one of the most important components of any training programme.

Health

As well as increasing your fitness, running improves your health.

Current best medical advice is that you should exercise for thirty minutes a day for three to four days a week.[2] This exercise should raise your heart rate to above 100 beats a minute, or to about 50–75 per cent of your maximum heart rate (see chapter 10 for a discussion about heart rates and exercise). Running regularly will increase your life expectancy and improve your quality of life.

Health benefits of running

Running has been shown to have the following health benefits:

- lower levels of body fat and obesity;
- lower risk of heart disease and stroke;
- stronger bones, reducing the risk of osteoporosis, osteoarthritis, etc.;
- reduced risk of diseases such as cancer and diabetes;
- improved immune system;
- stronger muscles, and less risk of degradation of joints;
- reduced risk of back pain;
- reduced incidence of depression and anxiety;
- increased co-ordination and mobility, especially in older adults.

Physical exercise is now recognised by the UK National Health Service as a major contributor to good health and an important focus for health promotion.[3] It is increasingly seen by the medical profession as one of the most cost-effective ways to improve the health status of the population.

Health risks from running

You may have been surprised by the suggestion that running can reduce the risk of damage to joints, since non-runners often claim that the opposite is true. Moreover, as your couch-potato friends probably point out to you, the legendary Jim Fixx, who kicked off the 1970s jogging craze in the US, died of a heart attack while out running. So what are the health risks associated with running?

The long-term impact of running on joints has not been especially well researched. Such evidence as there is suggests that people who have run consistently over many years have a lower risk in later life of joint problems such as arthritis than their sedentary counterparts.[4]

However, running is more likely to put stress on your joints than swimming, cycling or skiing, because of the repeated impact of hitting the ground. These risks can be reduced by using good quality and appropriate running shoes (see chapter 3), running on softer surfaces such as grass or trails when possible, and by starting running slowly.

As for the heart, the evidence is unambiguous: runners are less likely than non-runners to suffer from heart disease.[5] Admittedly, if a runner is going to have a heart attack (e.g. because of an inherited predisposition to heart disease) then it is more likely to happen while they are running than at other times of day, since this is when their heart is under most stress. It is true that Jim Fixx died of heart disease at the relatively young age of 51. But before he began jogging he had been a heavy smoker, and he had very high blood cholesterol. Jim Fixx survived longer than his father, who died from a heart attack at the age of 43; and the likelihood is that regular exercise lengthened Jim Fixx's life.[6]

Weight loss

Running is an excellent way to achieve lower levels of body fat and improved physical appearance.

The obesity epidemic

In England, the statistics are alarming. According to the National Audit Office, one in five adults is obese, and two-thirds of men and half of women are overweight, causing about 30,000 premature deaths a year in the UK alone. Treating obesity costs the NHS at least £0.5 billion a year. The wider costs to the economy in lower productivity and lost output are estimated to be a further £2 billion each year. Nearly three in five adults, about 20 million people, need a change in lifestyles.[7]

It is not necessary to accept the stereotyped images of models portrayed in the media (many of whom are below their most healthy body weight) to recognise that many people in rich countries (and increasingly in developing countries too) would be better off if they were less fat. Losing weight would improve their health, quality of life and life expectancy, and increase their self-esteem and enjoyment of life.

Poor diet, especially processed and intensively produced food, and lack of exercise, are contributing to a major epidemic of obesity that is rapidly becoming the most important health challenge facing the world.

According to the World Health Organisation,

'*the spectrum of problems seen in both developing and developed countries is having so negative an impact that obesity should be regarded as today's principal neglected public health problem*'.[8]

Running to lose weight

As we shall see in chapter 6, running is an excellent way to lose weight, reduce body fat and improve your physical appearance. If you eat more calories than you use, your

'It is a simple choice. Either I diet, and feel hungry all the time. Or I run regularly, eat exactly what I want, and still control my weight. I feel good about myself.'

Laura, runner for 6 years

body will store the extra energy as fat. So to lose weight, you have to burn more calories than you eat. Running is an excellent way to increase the calories you use.

Many runners find that, as their lifestyle becomes healthier, their choice of foods changes naturally and they instinctively begin to prefer more nutritious foods. So while they may still enjoy the occasional blow-out on a tub of ice cream or a plate of fast food, they know that they can do this now and again without feeling too guilty or hating themselves.

As we shall see, exercise provides a much more positive framework for weight loss than dieting. While dieters often feel perpetually unsatisfied, and suffer from a negative self-image, runners usually benefit from a continuing sense of achievement, self-confidence, and a weight level that can be sustained in the long term without continuing self-denial.

The mental benefits of running

In addition to the health and weight benefits of running, there is good evidence for the psychological benefits of exercise in general, and running in particular. Surveys have shown a strong correlation between being fit and being happy.[9] Exercise reduces anxiety levels and has been found to reduce depression (gentle running is now sometimes prescribed to patients with mild depressive symptoms). Some studies have shown that exercise increases mental performance and creative thinking.

Studies of the correlation between exercise and personality produce some striking results. Healthy adults who exercise regularly have greater energy, patience, humour, ambition, emotional stability, imagination, self-sufficiency and optimism, and are more amiable, graceful, good-tempered, elated and easy-going than similar people who don't exercise.[10]

Of course, these studies don't prove that exercise helps people to have these characteristics. It might be that people who already have these characteristics are more likely to exercise. Scientists don't know yet exactly how physical exercise reduces

> 'Running is "my time". It's the only time I don't have to give to my boss, my husband, or my daughters. It keeps me sane.'
>
> *Charlotte, mother of two, marketing manager and superwoman*

stress in a physical way. There are chemicals – called endorphins – that are produced during exercise and appear to reduce stress. (These chemicals are also responsible for the sensation known as 'runners' high'.) The faster metabolism and more effective cardiovascular systems of fit people also appear to contribute to their mental well-being.

As well as reducing stress through its physical effects, running also creates a space in which we can get time away from sources of anxiety and pressure. As George Sheehan vividly portrayed, runners are better able to cope with the pressures of everyday life, partly by permitting a different perspective on minor problems.

Many runners value their running because it gives them time alone, away from the pressures of work or family life. For them, there may be a simple pleasure in watching a city awake as dawn breaks; or enjoying a a run after work, perhaps as the sun goes down, or in the dark, as a way to shake off the stress of the day.

> 'Running is the physical break between my work world and my evening that allows me to have personal time with my family and friends.'
>
> *Phil McCubbins*

Conclusion

I have a busy and pressured job. My colleagues often ask me how I have so much energy. They think that because I have an active lifestyle as well as a demanding career, I should be perpetually tired. The truth is the opposite. My running gives me both physical and mental energy, and the confidence to juggle a busy life.

I generally run in the mornings, because that way I know that there will be no unexpected demands that will intervene to stop me running. If I try to run after work, I often find I cannot get away from the office in time. I also keep my running kit and shoes in my office, ready for a spare hour when I can go for a short run during the day (I am lucky enough to have shower facilities in my office).

Taking up running is a challenge at first. Stick at it: after a while it will become easier, and eventually it will become a natural and rewarding part of your life. As a fellow runner, I hope that this book will help you to test your own limits and find your own inner strengths.

2 First steps

Every runner was once a beginner. You should not feel that the rest of us were born with running shoes on, and that you have missed your chance. There is no 'too late' to start running, and many regular runners take it up in their forties or later. Running is simple, cheap and easy, while at the same time being one of the best ways yet invented to get fit, lose weight, improve your self-confidence and meet new friends.

'The miracle isn't that I finished ... The miracle is that I had the courage to start'.

John Bingham

Getting started

One of the great advantages of running as a sport is that you don't need much to get started. There is no significant equipment to buy (in the next chapter we shall look at buying running shoes and a sports bra). Nor is there a difficult technique to master. You don't have to find a group of people to run with (though you may want to do this later on) and you can run at any time of day that suits you. The only thing necessary to start running is for you to decide that it is what you want to do.

You may meet runners from time to time who began running at school, and perhaps were track stars or cross-country champions, and who have kept it up ever since. But the majority of the runners have taken it up later in life, often in their thirties or forties. Some runners begin when they retire from work. They universally find that running gives them a new hobby, new friends and a whole new outlook on life.

'Running is a great way to get to know a city! Not only do you get to meet some of the locals but by running through the streets, you learn your way around and even find some cool places you never knew existed! Both of these aspects help to make you feel part of the city!'.

Kathleen Broekhof, 28, from Toronto

Seeking medical advice

Do I need to see a doctor?

In an ideal world, everyone who takes up running should check with a doctor that they are not going to put themselves in danger. But for most runners this is unnecessary. According to the American Heart Association, you should ask yourself a number of questions, set out in the box.

In my view, you should also see a doctor in advance of running if you are significantly overweight (that is, if you have a Body Mass Index over 30 – see chapter 6), or if you might be pregnant. Use your common sense, and if you are in doubt, go to your doctor.

Should you see a doctor?

See your doctor if any of these apply to you:

- Your doctor said you have a heart condition and recommended only medically supervised physical activity.
- During or right after you exercise, you frequently have pains or pressure in the left or mid-chest area, left neck, shoulder or arm.
- You have developed chest pain within the last month.
- You tend to lose consciousness or fall over due to dizziness.
- You feel extremely breathless after mild exertion.
- Your doctor recommended you take medicine for your blood pressure or a heart condition.
- Your doctor said you have bone or joint problems that could be made worse by the proposed physical activity.
- You have a medical condition or other physical reason not mentioned here which might need special attention in an exercise programme (for example, insulin-dependent diabetes).
- You are middle-aged or older, have not been physically active, and plan a relatively vigorous exercise programme.

If none of these is true for you, you can start on a gradual, sensible programme of increased activity tailored to your needs. If you feel any of the physical symptoms listed above when you start your exercise programme, contact your doctor right away. If one or more of the above is true for you, an exercise-stress test may be used to help plan an exercise programme.

American Heart Association Exercise (Physical Activity) AHA Scientific Position, 1999

Do I need to see a physiotherapist?

Less obvious than seeing a doctor, you should also consider seeing a sports physiotherapist before beginning a running programme. A physio can help to identify features of your running style that could eventually, if you run regularly, lead to an injury. For more information about physiotherapy, see chapter 8.

Starting out

So you've decided to start running, and you've taken medical advice if you need it. You've jumped ahead to chapter 3 and bought yourself running shoes and a sports bra. Now what?

If you are completely new to running, you should not try to do too much at first. A common error is to think that you should run flat out. As we'll see in the training plan later in this chapter, you should begin by walking, in order to get used to being on your feet. You should build up to running over several weeks, and then only for a few minutes at a time.

At this stage in your running, you should stick rigorously to the **talk test**: if you cannot talk in complete sentences during your training runs, you are running too fast.

Avoiding injury when you start running

Experience shows that many people who are new to running end up with minor injuries in the first six months of running. These injuries are frequently related to trying to do too much, or having the wrong shoes. For many runners, injury comes just at the time when they are beginning to love their new sport, and it can be very frustrating to have to ease off or stop completely.

It is sensible to start running for short times and distances at first, and then gradually build up. The reason for this is that your body takes time to adapt to running. When you start to run, your cardiovascular fitness increases, your muscles become stronger, and your joints and ligaments adapt to the impact of daily running. But your overall fitness level and energy can increase faster than your joints have adapted. If you get carried away, you may start to run longer and faster before your joints and ligaments are really ready, with the result that you may injure yourself. In one study of reasonably fit people who started to run *almost all* of them became injured at some time in the third month of training.[11] These problems are entirely avoidable, with just a little patience and willingness to learn from experience.

How to avoid injury when you begin

- if you are new to running, walk for the first month;
- build up slowly; never increase your weekly mileage by more than two miles or 10 per cent, whichever is greater;
- get proper running shoes from a specialist running shop;
- run on grass or trails rather than roads and pavements if possible;
- get advice from experienced runners;
- ignore the feeling in your first three months that you could be doing more;
- see a physiotherapist to get advice on how you might improve your running style.

In order to avoid injury, you need to hold back from running too much at first even if you feel ready to go further and faster. In particular, it is a good idea to start off with a month of brisk walking, rather than running. This helps your body to adapt to the effect of regular impact of your feet on the ground, before you start to increase your running mileage.

One perennial problem is the runners who decide (often as a New Year resolution) that they are going to run a marathon. At my running club we get a huge influx of runners every January who have decided to train for the London Marathon, which is in April. By March, many of them have dropped out through injury. Four months is simply too short to train for a marathon. First-timers would be much better off building up more slowly, perhaps running a half marathon later in the year, and aiming for a marathon the following year.

At the end of this chapter we'll have a look at a training programme to get you started safely from scratch.

Where to run

If you are new to running, one of the first challenges is to figure out where you can run.

Look at a map of your local area, and see what there is in the way of green spaces, such as parks. There are often footpaths alongside rivers and canals. If you know a nearby cycling shop, you may be able to buy a map that shows cycling routes, which are often suitable for running.

There may be running routes for your area on the internet (the Serpentine website[12] has some suggested routes in the London area). There may also be a book with routes for running or walking near you.

Best of all, members of your local running club will know running routes in your area. (See p. 38 on running safely.)

How to measure the distances of your routes

There are several ways to measure the distances of your running routes:

- if the route is on roads, you may be able to drive a **car** round them and use the car's distance meter;
- if you have a bike with a **cycling computer**, you can use this to measure the distance;
- use a **map**, and either a roller-wheel (which you can buy in a good map shop), which you roll along the route on the map to measure the distance, or a piece of string;
- use an **electronic map from the internet**, and software such as AccuRoute which measures the distance between points on a map on a computer;[13]
- use a modern **pedometer**, which measures your distance accurately (see chapter 3).

Running to and from work

One way to introduce running into a busy life is to run to or from work, or even both. Whether this works for you depends on the distance, and whether you have facilities at work for showering and changing. Some runners keep a selection of clean clothes in the office, which they refresh once a week on their rest day, taking home the week's dirty clothes.

Running to work: the tale of Roger Matthews

'I recall a mediocre athlete many years ago . . . His coach told him he should go for the 10 km event, but the mileage the coach asked him to do was so extensive that the athlete, a carpenter by trade, who travelled long distances to work, could not fit it in. The answer was to run to and from work. However, at the time, his work-site was 15 miles away. He was undaunted by the prospect and ran the 30 miles involved daily, five days a week. He rested Saturday and Sunday. This athlete, Roger Matthews, became the 4th fastest 10 km runner in the world in 1970.'

Frank Horwill, UK Athletics Coach and
founder of the British Milers Club

If you can figure out the logistics, you may well find that running to work is the best way to fit running into your day. Often it does not take any more time than travelling on public transport or driving. If you have a long journey, you may find that you can run to or from a railway station or bus stop that is one stop further away from your home.

There are several rucksacks available that are designed for wearing while running. These have chest straps and compression straps to reduce bounce. Visit a local specialist running shop to see what is available. You might also want to invest in a travel towel, which is like a chamois leather and light and easy to carry, and is available from most camping shops.

Goals and motivation

The nature of our goals defines what sort of runner we are. You may want to lose some weight or increase your fitness, to reduce stress and increase your self-confidence, or you may want to achieve a particular time in a race. Effective goal-setting is an important part of increasing your motivation and commitment to running, and getting the most out of the sport.

How to set good goals

Your goal should be achievable but challenging. It should be specific, positive, and tied to a particular timeframe. A good goal might be 'lose 5 kg in six months'. A goal such as 'lose some weight' is not sufficiently specific and will not motivate you in the same way. Your goals might be a mixture of longer-term objectives, over a period of months, and shorter-term goals over the coming weeks.

'Enter a race for motivation. When you start it can sometimes be difficult to keep motivated, especially when it's cold or wet, but if you have a definite target in the form of a race it can be a lot easier. I was a jogger for years, never really improving because I would only go running intermittently, until I entered my first race. Now I race regularly and think of myself as a runner, not a jogger.'

Paul Curd, 46, sub-4-hour marathon runner

If your main goal is a long way off – such as completing a marathon in nine months' time – you should set yourself some intermediate targets, for example completing a particular 10 km course or a half marathon. These intermediate targets should be measurable and time-bound.

If you are not sure what goal to set yourself for a race, seek advice from more experienced runners about what you might realistically achieve. The race time predictor table in chapter 11 may also be useful to help you to extrapolate from your times at other distances.

Visualise what it will be like to achieve your goal. Promise yourself a reward when you achieve it. Write your goals down, and tell your friends and family about them. This will help to maintain your commitment. You may want to stick a reminder on the fridge.

One of the best ways to motivate yourself is to team up with a friend and agree to do something together. You might both agree to run the same race, for example. Supporting each other will help to reinforce your goal.

Don't become obsessive, or put your goal above your family, friends or health.

Review your goals regularly and adjust them if necessary. If you are injured before your marathon and cannot safely take part, then adjust your goal. You can always take part in another race in the future. Having the wisdom to know when you should adjust your goal is just as important as having the courage and tenacity to overcome challenges on the way.

Training logs

A training log is a diary where you write down every run that you do. Although it may sound ludicrously geeky if you have never done it, keeping a training log is one of the best ways to keep motivated as a runner. A log will help you to track your progress, and to stick to your training programme. Over time, it will be a useful source of information to trace the origins of a period of good running, or of injury and boredom.

What to record in a training log

In a training log, you might record:

- how far you ran;
- the time you ran for;
- the time of day you ran;
- where you ran;
- how you felt (perhaps on a scale of 1–5);
- which shoes you were wearing (to track how many miles the shoes have done so that you know when to replace them);
- your average and peak heart rate (if you measure it);
- any other special factors.

Some people also record the weather conditions, their weight, how much sleep they had, who they ran with, their menstrual cycle, and so on.

How to keep a training log

Lots of people keep their log in a notebook, or in their diary. This is often the simplest solution. For more technically minded runners, you can also use an electronic diary, such as a palm-top; or use a spreadsheet on your PC.

There is also a wide range of bespoke software available on the internet designed for athletes to track their running, which runs on personal computers. Of these, RunLog[14] and The Training Diary[15] are both particularly good.

Finally, there are an increasing number of websites that you can use to record your training online, some of which provide links to advice by coaches. There is an index of running log software on the internet at <www.serpentine.org.uk/software/>

Joining a running club

One of the great things about running is that you can do it alone. Many of us enjoy running precisely because it gives us a little time to ourselves. But there are also significant benefits from being a member of a running club. Running clubs are not full of super-fit, super-fast athletes; nor are they full of serious runners. You don't have to get fast before you join: whatever your standard, you will be welcome, and you will almost certainly find that there are plenty of members who run more slowly than you do. Running clubs are generally quite cheap (they cost upwards of £10 a year).

'There are all sorts of running clubs, just as there are all sorts of runners. I once belonged to a very serious club, full of really serious athletes who all wanted to win every race. I remember preparing for a race where all the runners from my club were warming up alone, focusing on the race ahead, while a group from another club were limbering up together, chatting and laughing, and seemed to be having FUN. I decided there and then to join that club. So my advice would be to enter a few races and check out which clubs have runners who seem to be on your wavelength.'

Paul Curd (now a member of the Serpentine Running Club)

Meeting for a club run

Why join a running club?

There are a number of benefits from joining a running club:

- by arranging to meet with other runners, you will be encouraged to **run regularly**, and this will make it easier to continue running;
- you'll get **advice from experienced runners** on how to start running, how to avoid injury, how to improve, good routes to run in your area, how to enter events, how to run at different speeds and over different distances, and so on;
- you will get **motivation and enjoyment** from running with other people, and you will find that the miles slip past on your long runs as you chat with new friends;
- you will **meet people** with a similar passion for exercise and running;
- you get **discounts at running shops** and on race entries.

Depending on the club, you may also get access to coaching, regular races and competition (if you want it) and an opportunity to be part of a team. Some clubs provide access to physiotherapy, and information such as newsletters and seminars.

Am I too slow for a running club?

Many new runners feel they should wait until they are faster and more experienced before they join a club. This is a mistake. Many clubs will have one or two fast megastars, but these will easily be outnumbered by members who run to control stress, keep fit, lose weight or just to socialise. Don't be daunted about joining a club. Every one of its members has been a beginner at some time. Any club will be excited to welcome new people into the sport.

What does a running club actually do?

Running clubs vary. Most are focused on regular weekly club runs, often with a social element. Some organise track training sessions and coaching, liaise with the national athletics organisation (UK Athletics in Britain), inform members about events and

Questions to ask when you join a running club

Any club worth joining will welcome visitors – just show up for one of their runs and see if you like it. Here are some questions you might ask yourself:

- Where are they based? How hard is it to get to the meeting point from home or work? Are the runs somewhere pleasant?
- What are the facilities like? Do they have changing facilities or a clubhouse?
- How serious is the club? Some clubs tend to be quite serious, some less competitive. Is it too competitive for you? Not serious enough?
- What sort of running do they do? Do they do road running, marathons, cross-country and track and field? Which are you interested in?
- When are their club runs? Are they at a convenient time? Are they on a convenient day of the week?
- What sort of people are they? Will you enjoy spending time with them? Do they organise social events?
- How much does it cost?

races, enter teams in team events such as relays, provide information to members, arrange social events, and organise races. Most of all, they link runners with other runners.

The Serpentine Running Club – Central London's Running Club

I am a member of the Serpentine Running Club, which is based in London's Hyde Park. Because of its location, it attracts a lot of young people working in London, including a lot of visitors to London from overseas. Unusually for a running club, about half the members are women.

There are club runs on Wednesdays and Saturdays, track sessions on Tuesdays and Thursdays, and long runs on Sunday mornings. Club members also organise weekend bike rides, yoga sessions, swimming classes, triathlon training and seminars. There are weekend races, and the club organises excursions for events such as the Davos Marathon in Switzerland, the Welsh Castles Relay, and trips to marathons in Paris, Berlin, Boston, Amsterdam and New York.

Membership of the Serpentine Running Club costs £20 a year (half price for pensioners, free for students). This allows you 10% off your kit from London running shops, discounts on race entry, insurance, a quarterly newsletter, as well as an active social life.

For more information, have a look at the website at <www.serpentine.org.uk>.

How do I find a good club?

Probably the best place to get information about running clubs is from a local specialist running shop. You can also get contact details from UK Athletics, or on the internet.

> 'My running club is the only reason I stay here. It is the best way to meet people of all different ages, from every walk of life.'
>
> *Simon, 30, from New Zealand*

Entering races

It often comes as a surprise to new runners that races are not especially competitive. There may be half a dozen runners or so who are in contention to win the race; for the rest of us, races are a way to challenge ourselves, measure our performance, run with other people, and benefit from the race facilities such as traffic-free roads and water tables. The camaraderie among the runners creates a great atmosphere of mutual support. In short, races are a good day out. As we shall see in chapter 11, you don't need to be especially fast to enter a race.

One of the great merits of running, compared with other sports, is that you can enter the same competition as world-class athletes, whatever your level.

Races, teams and clubs

Many races give prizes for teams as well as individuals. These are calculated by adding up the position or time of a number of team members, and awarding the prize to the team with the lowest aggregate. Running clubs don't choose team members in advance: it is simply the first members of the club to finish who score (e.g. the first four). This means that you don't have to be 'selected' to run for your club. In most races you must be wearing your club's shirt to score for your club.

A training programme for beginners

'My advice to new runners? Get a running buddy.'

Al Chou, cyclist and sub-3-hour marathon runner

Before you start

The training programme shown at table 2.1 is designed for a complete beginner to get from couch potato to running 10–20 miles a week, over a period of six months.

Before you start this training programme, you should have:

- checked whether you need **advice from a doctor** (see page 8);
- bought yourself proper **running shoes** and, if you are a woman, a **sports bra** (see chapter 3).

In addition, you should remember that:

- it is a good idea to **find a mate** who wants to do this with you, so that you can encourage each other; alternatively, start going along to a local running club;
- set yourself a **goal** – such as a 5 km race – which you can work towards;
- the first few weeks of this programme may well seem rather boring and easy, but you should **resist the temptation to go any further or faster** so that you avoid injury. This programme lays a solid foundation for safe, healthy running in the future;
- if you find that you are not enjoying it for the first few weeks, **stick with it**. It often takes three to four weeks to really get into running (or to get back into it). For most people, there will suddenly come a time when you realise that it has become easy, and that you really enjoy it.

Table 2.1 Training programme for a complete beginner

Week	Mon	Tues	Wed	Thur	Fri	Sat	Sun
1	← Walk for 20 minutes every other day →						
2	← Walk for 20 minutes every other day →						
3	W20	W20	–	W20	–	W20	–
4	–	W20.R5	–	W20	–	W20	–
5	–	W20.R5	–	W20	–	W15.R5	–
6	W10	W20.R5	–	W15.R5	–	W15.R5	–
7	W5.R5	W15.R5	–	W15.R5	–	W15.R5	–
8	W5.R5	W20.R5	–	W15.R5	–	W20.R5	–
9	W5.R5	W10.R10	–	W10.R10	–	W15.R10	–
10	W5.R10	W20.R10	–	W20.R10	–	W20.R10	–
11	W10.R10	W15.R15	–	W15.R10	–	W15.R10	–
12	W10.R10	W15.R15	–	W15.R15	–	W15.R10	–
13	W15.R10	W10.R20	–	W15.R15	–	W15.R10	–
14	W10.R15	W10.R20	–	W10.R20	R10.W10	W10.R20	–
15	W5.R15	W5.R25	–	W5.R25	–	W10.R10	–
16	W5.R20	R30	–	W5.R20	R30	W5.R15	–
17	R25	R30	–	R20	R30	R20	–
18	R30	R30	–	R20	R30	R25	–
19	R30	R30	–	R25	R30	R25	–
20	R20	R30	–	R20	–	R20	–
21	R30	R30	–	R30	R25	R20	–
22	R30	R35	–	R30	R30	R25	–
23	R30	R40	–	R30	R30	R30	–
24	R20	R45	–	R20	R30	R30	–

Legend: W10 = Walk for 10 minutes. R10 = Run for 10 minutes

About the programme

The numbers shown in the table are *minutes* a day. (They are not miles!) These are intended to give you an idea of how long you should be exercising. It does not matter how *fast* you go at this stage.

The training programme begins with just walking for the first three weeks. Don't take this too easily: it should be brisk walking, so that you are breathing heavily and perhaps sweating a little. The purpose of the three weeks of walking is to stimulate your bones, muscles and joints to adapt to the exercise, so that they are ready for when you start running.

Over the next three weeks, we add in an extra five-minute run for each week, for the last five minutes of the walk. Then over the next two months, the amount of running gradually increases, and the walking reduces, so that by week 16 you can do two thirty-minute runs.

It is a common mistake to try to run too fast. Remember the **talk test**: you should be able to maintain a conversation easily, in complete sentences, on all these runs. If you are too out of breath to speak easily, you are running too fast.

Conclusion

Your first steps as a runner are the most important. They will determine whether running becomes a lifelong pleasure, or a temporary, injury-laden aberration. Once you lace up a pair of running shoes and get outside, you will find that it is much easier, and more rewarding, than you imagined it could be. The biggest obstacle is likely to be that you try to do too much too soon.

Somewhere near you there is a community of runners, each of whom was once a beginner. If you want to sustain running as part of your lifestyle, learn from the experience of others, and enjoy a broader social life, you should consider linking up with colleagues or friends who run, or joining a local running club. Summon up the courage to go along: it is a decision you will never regret.

Celebrities at the Race for Life 5 km

3 Shoes and kit

One of the benefits of running as a sport is that you won't need to invest much in kit and accessories.

All you really need is a decent pair of running shoes and (if you are a woman) a well-designed sports bra. Given how little you need for the sport, it would be a huge mistake to think that you can get by without either of these. Of course, if you enjoy accessorising and want to spend lots of money on clothes and other kit, there is plenty of running-related paraphernalia you can buy. This chapter tells you how to go about it.

What shoes to buy

There is no such thing as a better 'make' or 'model' of shoes. A good pair of running shoes is one that suits your particular running style; and a bad pair is one that does not.

Biomechanics and shoes

The human body generally comes with complicated machinery – muscles, tendons, ligaments, joints, bones – to enable you to walk and run. Your ability to run efficiently and injury-free depends in part on the alignment and operation of these moving parts. Your individual *biomechanics* are partly determined by your genes, but also by your lifestyle, past injuries, treatment and exercises. Running shoes vary according to the way and extent to which they compensate for faulty biomechanics, and your choice of running shoes should depend on your personal biomechanical profile.

Paradoxically, the best runners often don't need to spend much money on running shoes. Because they are typically blessed with good biomechanics, their running style does not require them to buy shoes that correct the way in which their feet roll when they hit the ground, or cushion them from the stress on their joints as their feet repeatedly hit the ground. The rest of us mere mortals, however, need shoes that will correct our deficiencies and weaknesses, and improve our running action so that every footstep does not place an intolerable pressure on our feet, legs and pelvis.

Pronation and supination

When your heel hits the ground, the foot naturally rolls in from the outside edge. This rolling is called **pronation**, and is a natural and desirable part of the running action, since it helps to absorb the impact of running (rather like a parachutist bending her knees and rolling as she hits the ground).

Although some pronation is desirable, around three-quarters of runners 'overpronate' – that is, their feet roll in too much. This is most visible in the effect it has further up the leg, as the knee tends to bend in across the centre of the body towards the other leg. Persistent overpronation may cause a variety of injuries: stress in the ankle and Achilles tendon, shin splints, knee pain, torn hamstrings, hip strains, or pain in the lower back. These injuries are discussed in more detail in chapter 8.

Just before the take-off phase of running, the foot rolls back towards the outside. This is called **supination**. As with pronation, this is a normal part of the running action. But a small minority of the population – less than 10 per cent – oversupinate. This can also cause a range of overuse injuries over time.

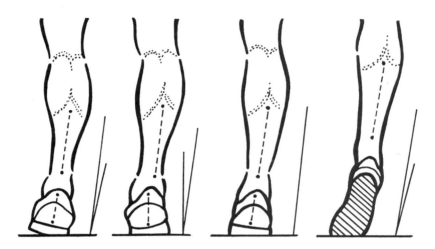

Phases of foot strike

Excessive pronation and supination may be caused in part by problems in the feet; but they are usually also symptoms of imbalances or weaknesses elsewhere in the body, including in the back, hips, buttocks, hamstrings, quadriceps and knees. While the right running shoes can help to limit the effect of these biomechanical deficiencies, it is better if possible to identify and correct the underlying causes.

Runners who are lucky enough neither to pronate nor supinate excessively are called 'neutral'. They don't need special shoes to correct their gait (i.e. their running style) – though shoes that are designed to prevent overpronation are unlikely to do them any harm – which often means that they can wear lighter and cheaper shoes than their less fortunate brethren.

A simple check for overpronation

1. Stand in front of a full-length mirror, barefoot, on one leg, with your hands behind your back, and your toes facing forwards;
2. Keeping your pelvis level and your back straight, slowly bend the leg on which you are standing;
3. Your knee should go straight forwards, over your second toe. If it bends in towards the other leg, past the big toe, then you probably over-pronate when you run.

Front View   *Side View*

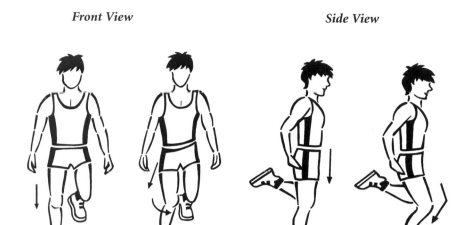

Correct alignment   Pronation knee inwards

Checking for overpronation

Motion control and stability

Because most of the population overpronates, most running shoes are designed to prevent or at least limit overpronation. A simple test to see how much a shoe prevents overpronation is to hold the toe in one hand, and the heel in the other, and twist the shoe. The more difficult it is to twist, the more the shoe will help to control overpronation.

Running shoes come in the following categories:

- **Motion control**:
  most aggressive at preventing overpronation.
- **Stability**:
  help to limit overpronation, but not as much as motion control.
- **Neutral**:
  for runners who don't need their shoes to prevent biomechanical weaknesses.
- **Supinators**:
  for the minority of the population who oversupinate.

These running shoes all look basically the same at first, but when you look at them carefully they have different components built into the shoe according to the extent to which they are designed to control pronation.

Cushioning

As well as controlling the rotation of the foot and ankle, running shoes vary in the extent to which they cushion the foot as it hits the ground. Good cushioning is important because it reduces the shock that is transmitted through the foot to the lower leg, knee and hip joints. As well as reducing the risk of injury, cushioning

'When I first started running, I used a pair of old plimsolls. It did my knees no good whatsoever. I recommend that you go to a good running shop and get a decent pair of trainers.'

Malcolm French, Serpentine Men's Captain

improves the comfort of running. Heavier runners, and those doing big mileages on roads or pavements, should ensure that their running shoes have sufficient cushioning.

However, cushioning makes the shoe heavier, and because it absorbs energy it can reduce your running efficiency. For most of us the effect on performance is imperceptible; and the benefit of more comfort and safety when running more than outweighs the loss of performance. But some runners will also use **racing flats** for important races (see below).

Different manufacturers have different cushioning technologies. Some use pockets of air to absorb impact; others use gels or spongy plastics. You should try these for yourself and see which you find most comfortable.

Other types of shoe

As well as regular trainers, other running shoes available include:

- **racing flats**

  These are basically trainers that have very little cushioning, and usually not much motion control, but they are correspondingly lighter than shoes you might use for regular training. Unless you are very concerned about your performance, or have very good biomechanics, racing flats are generally best left to the professional athletes.

- **track spikes**

  These are for training on the athletics track. They have short spikes under the toes that grip the track. The shape of the shoe forces you to run on your toes, which is more efficient on short distances (though harder on your legs). Track spikes have very little cushioning or motion control.

- **cross-country spikes**

  These have longer spikes than track shoes, designed to give you more traction on soft ground; like track shoes they have little cushioning because they are usually used on softer ground and because the lack of cushioning gives them more stability on uneven ground. They also have little motion control. Because of the spikes, they cannot be used on hard surfaces. The spikes are replaceable, and different length spikes are used depending on the nature of the surface.

- **fell shoes**

  These are designed for running off road, for example on mountain trails; they usually have good grips on the bottom of the shoe, such as studs. Like cross country spikes, they generally have little cushioning and motion control, because they are designed for use on softer, uneven ground.

These specialist running shoes are not generally available in high-street sports shops. For a good selection, and good advice, you should go to a specialist running store, where you will be given individual advice on your needs.

How long do shoes last?

You often see people looking at the bottom of a running shoe to see if it needs replacing, for example by seeing whether it has much 'tread' left. This is a mistake: the main determinant of the longevity of a shoe is not the extent of wear to the outer sole; it is the compression of the mid-sole, which is the spongy layer between the outer sole and your feet. Most running shoes today have an EVA mid-sole.[16] EVA is light and absorbs shock well, but it gradually compacts as it is used, which reduces its shock absorbency and gradually distorts the shoe. As a result of the compression of the mid-sole most running shoes have an average life expectancy of about 300–600 miles.

> 'Buy a new pair of shoes every 300 miles or so: in the end it will save you money because you won't have to pay out a lot of money for physio treatment.'
>
> *Rachel Broster*

Very heavy or uneven runners might wear out part of the outer sole before the mid-sole is too compressed, but this is unlikely.

The actual life of your shoes depends on your weight and your running style. You can see whether your shoes are past their best by looking at the compression lines along the side of the shoe, and seeing whether the mid-sole can be compressed with pressure from your thumb. If you can no longer compress the mid-sole, then it is time to replace the shoes. If you begin to get any kind of ache or pain in your ankle or knee, check that your running shoes don't need replacing.

Incidentally, you should *not* put your running shoes in the washing machine, nor use very hot water to clean them. The hot water damages the shoe, especially the mid-sole, and leads to distortion in the shape of the shoe.

Many runners keep track of the life of their running shoes in their training log, and use this to warn them when they are likely to need a new pair.

How many pairs of shoes do I need?

Most runners will do fine with a single pair of training shoes. However, if you are going to run track or cross-country regularly, you should consider getting a pair of specialist shoes for this too (see page 23).

Some runners have two pairs of trainers at the same time, and alternate between them. The reasons for this are:

- it is claimed that both pairs of shoes last longer than they would do if they were used one at a time, because they benefit from the 'rest' between runs;
- the two pairs of shoes will be slightly different (even if they are the same model they will wear slightly differently), which marginally reduces the risk of injury, because there is more variation in the way you run;
- if a pair of shoes gets wet, you can use the other pair while the first pair dries out;
- when you find a model of shoe that suits you, the shoe manufacturers may discontinue it, so you might as well buy two pairs of a shoe you like.

Where to buy running shoes

You should buy running shoes from a specialist running shop if possible. At a good running shop, the staff will help you to pick shoes that fit your own running style and help to control your biomechanical weaknesses. They may have specialist equipment for this (e.g. a treadmill with sensors to detect how your feet hit the ground) or they may watch you run up and down the street outside.

Such shops are often a little more expensive than high-street stores, but they usually offer discounts to members of running clubs on production of a membership card. However, their staff are much more knowledgeable and patient than your average teenager in a Saturday job; and they are usually runners themselves. Also, it is a false economy to save a few pounds on running shoes if the result is that you get a pair that are not right for you, and end up injured.

Try to go to the running shop in the afternoon, when your feet are larger than in the morning; and pick a quiet time (e.g. mid-afternoon on a weekday) when the staff will have time to help you choose the right shoes. If they are not willing to let you try out the shoes, and watch you to see how you run in them, shop somewhere else.

You will find the details of running shops in running magazines, or on the internet; or your local running club will be able to advise you on where you can go.

If you run high mileages and you are prone to running injuries, you may want to get advice from a podiatrist on the best pair of shoes for you (see chapter 8).

Clothing

You don't need to rush out and buy a whole new wardrobe of running gear. But if you run regularly, you are likely to end up buying clothes specifically for running.

Sports bras

All women should wear sports bras when they run. The *Cooper's Ligaments* that support the breasts can be permanently stretched and damaged if the breasts are not properly supported during exercise. This leads to droopy breasts, and cannot be reversed. A good sports bra provides support for your breasts to prevent them from bouncing while you run. In addition, surveys show that half of women who exercise suffer from breast pain, and this is an important reason why some of them give up.

Sports bras essentially work in two, different (not necessarily mutually exclusive) ways:

- they compress your breasts against your body, to reduce the bounce; and/or
- they individually cup each breast, and so provide each breast with support.

It is often said that women with large cup sizes prefer sports bras that support each breast individually, while women with small cup sizes prefer sports bras that simply compress the breasts. This preference is not universal, however – and was not borne

'The right sports bra for you is one that fits you comfortably and significantly reduces the movement of your bust when running. Every woman's bust is different, so what works for your training partner, may not be right for you.'

Selaine Messem, owner, <www.lessbounce.com>

out at all in my (admittedly unscientific) survey of women runners whom I asked about this.

The best way to choose a sports bra is to get expert advice. There are now specialist retailers in the UK such as www.lessbounce.com who can talk you through the details by phone or by email.

You should not buy your bra based on a measurement of your bust size. Bras from different manufacturers are not all the same size. Your measurement may have been done badly, or your bust size may have changed (especially if you increase your training, which tends to reduce your cup size). Your optimal fitting can also vary over your menstrual cycle (because of water retention). Instead you should try the bra and choose one that is comfortable for you and that fits you snugly. Check that there are no seams or clips that will irritate your skin over a long run. Jump up and down – your breasts should hardly bounce at all. Make sure that the base of the bra will not ride up over your breasts while you are running, but that it is not so tight that it is difficult to breathe easily. You should also find out whether the shoulder straps cut in.

After running, particularly on long runs, some women have sore skin either between the breasts, across the back under the strap and buckle, or along the line of the base of the bra under the breasts. This friction can be reduced by liberal application of Vaseline, or some other lubricant, on these areas before you start running.

A *crop top* is not the same as a sports bra, and many of them don't provide the support you need. However, there are some sports bras that are designed to look like

crop tops so that you can run in them without a t-shirt over the top.

A number of manufacturers also make sports bras that are designed to accommodate the sensor strap of a heart rate monitor, to prevent you from having to have two separate straps around your chest.

Like running shoes, you need to replace your sports bras from time to time – with a lot of use they can last less than a year. Check regularly to see if your bust is moving more than it should, or if you are beginning to get breast pain. You may also find that your bra begins to rub after a while.

T-shirts and shorts

You'll need some shorts and t-shirts for running. At first you can just dig out some old summer clothes, but over time you may want to get some clothes specifically for running.

'Running in wet cotton t-shirts always rubs my nipples until they bleed, and I end up looking as if I've been in a road accident.'

Geoff Higham, 31

The most important lesson about buying clothes for running is to steer well clear of cotton. When cotton gets wet (from sweat, or from rain) it gets heavy, irritates the skin, does not insulate well and dries slowly.

Sports clothes manufacturers have come up with synthetic materials that *wick* away the moisture (that is, move the water from the surface near the skin to the outer layer where it can evaporate). Examples are Nike DriFit™ and Adidas Climalite™. Miraculously, these 'technical' materials really do help to keep you dry, warm in cold weather and cool in warm weather. They are also more expensive. The other main downside is that some runners find that they retain body odour more than other materials, even when washed.

For **t-shirts**, you will need some short-sleeved and long-sleeved shirts depending on the weather. If you use t-shirts made of technical materials, then don't wear a cotton t-shirt over the top, or underneath, for warmth, since this prevents the sweat from evaporating through the technical clothing. Instead, get a long-sleeved, thermal, technical top for running in the cold.

Your choice of **shorts** is a matter of personal preference. Some runners prefer to wear tight, Lycra™-style shorts (like cycling shorts but without the padding) because these reduce friction between the thighs. Others prefer baggier shorts. Lots of people wear both: the tight shorts underneath to reduce friction, with baggy shorts over the top – a combination that is less revealing but can get hot. If you are running in a foreign country, think about local sensibilities and customs before setting off in only a pair of skin-tight, figure-hugging cycling shorts.

You can also wear **running tights**, which may come down to your knees, calves or toes. These keep you warm in cold weather, and are sometimes worn by runners who prefer not to display their legs. Again, some runners accompany these with a pair of baggy shorts over the top.

Socks

You can also invest in **socks** that are specifically designed for running. You probably won't need these unless you run long distances. You may not notice a seam that rubs your feet over 5 or 10 miles. But by the end of a marathon, you will be painfully aware of every seam, and could well have blisters where your socks have rubbed.

Sock manufacturers such as Thorlos™ make socks that have no seams, and of which the soles are padded for comfort. I like these, but I know many runners who find them too warm. Other brands of socks are double-layered, which helps to reduce blisters (since the layers rub against each other, rather than against your skin). Many runners swear by these, others find them uncomfortable after they have first been washed. Try the different brands and see which suit you best.

Underwear

Men's running shorts usually include an inner liner, designed to support all their equipment, so men don't in general wear underpants under their running shorts.

Some women's shorts and running tights are lined and have proper gussets – these can be worn without knickers underneath if you want. Otherwise, there is often a seam just where you don't want it, which would be very uncomfortable without underwear. Many women wear knickers under their running shorts or tights in any case, for comfort or in case their shorts are otherwise too revealing (especially since some materials become quite see-through when wet).

When it is very cold, runners (of both sexes) sometimes wear thermal underwear under their shorts to keep all their parts warm. The key to good thermal underwear is that it should be windproof. Helly Hansen™ makes thermal underwear designed for sports, available in both men's and women's versions.

Clothes for cold weather

In cold weather, the best approach is to dress in many **light layers**. In general you should have a synthetic **base layer** that wicks sweat away from your skin, with a windproof or water-resistant **top layer**. On very cold days, you may need an additional **thermal layer** in between. Using layers enables you to keep warm with the least weight of clothes, and enables you to regulate your temperature quickly and easily by adding or removing layers as you want.

You may also want to use some light **gloves**. In general, the thin nylon type work well (cotton and woollen gloves are not sufficiently windproof and can become waterlogged). You can get gloves for runners which are fluorescent yellow, or which have reflective material for running in the dark.

For running when it is cold, you may want a **hat**. A regular woollen hat will do, or a baseball cap made of synthetic material. Again, you can get water resistant caps, which are useful if it is drizzling; and you can get bright and reflective hats which ensure that you are seen in traffic.

When you choose a **raincoat**, you will have to trade off three considerations: the extent to which the jacket is waterproof, its breathability (i.e. whether it retains your perspiration) and its weight. On the whole, jackets that are fully waterproof are heavy, and when you run in them you will become damp inside because your sweat does not

evaporate properly. But breathable jackets are rarely fully waterproof: they might protect you from a shower, but will not be much use in heavy rain.

I find that fully waterproof materials, such as Gore-Tex™, are too heavy for running. They are also insufficiently breathable, so that you get thoroughly wet inside them as your perspiration is retained. So I prefer a raincoat that is windproof and showerproof, but not fully waterproof. This helps to keep me warm in the rain, and I figure I'm going to get wet whatever happens.

One excellent option for bad weather is a **gillet**, which is a waistcoat-shaped jacket made from water-resistant material that protects your torso but not your arms. This can keep you warm in rain and wind, while allowing your sweat to evaporate. A **body-warmer** is a waistcoat-shaped thermal top for keeping your torso warm.

As well as a suitable jacket, many runners (male and female) use running tights for cold weather, long-sleeved thermal tops, and if necessary thermal underwear (see above).

> 'There is no such thing as bad weather for running: only the wrong clothing.'
>
> *Grethe Petersen, 34, club runner from Denmark*

Clothes for hot weather

In hot weather, you should **not** strip down to the bare minimum, because you must make sure that you protect your skin from the sun. **Sunscreen** can be annoying, because it blocks your pores and so prevents you from sweating, and also runs into your eyes, but it is a lot better than skin cancer. On long runs, remember to refresh your sunscreen regularly, in case it is being washed away by sweat. If possible, block the sun using a sunhat and t-shirt so that you don't have to rely on suntan lotion. Use zinc cream (much favoured by cricketers) to protect your face from the sun.

As for your clothes, technical t-shirts will wick sweat away, which will keep you cool and help to prevent sweat from irritating your skin.

Clothes for racing

In a race, you are working harder and producing more energy. In general, you should feel a bit cold when you line up at the start of a race. If you are not cold before the gun goes, you will probably be too warm once the race is under way.

Faster runners will almost always wear just shorts and a running vest in races. But in cold weather, many mid-pack runners in longer races wear a long-sleeved t-shirt, and perhaps running tights. Remember that you do produce a lot of heat when you are running, so you should be careful not to overheat.

One tip for racing is to take an unused **bin liner** with you, in which you cut holes for your head and arms. You can wear this while you are waiting for the race to start to keep warm and dry. Just before, or just after, the race begins, you can rip this off and throw it away on the side of the road (make sure that it does not obstruct other runners – put it in a bin if you can). This enables you to wear suitably cool clothes for the race, without getting too cold or wet before you start.

You should always have warm, dry clothes with you to change into after a long run or a race. As well as a dry t-shirt and tracksuit trousers, I like to have fresh socks and shoes to wear, to give my feet a rest. (See chapter 11 for more information about races.)

Timing and distance measurement

Watches

Most runners use a watch with a stopwatch function to measure how long they run. Look for a watch with the following features:

- a large display, so that you can see it while you are running, and a light so that you can see it in the dark;
- a stopwatch with a lap function, preferably one that can store 10 or more laps in its memory;
- water resistance, for running in the rain;
- easy-to-press buttons, so that you can press the lap button during a race or on the track.

A number of manufacturers make watches specifically designed for runners. The Nike Triax™ range is particularly popular, partly because of the shape of the strap which goes past the wrist bone; and Timex also make Ironman Triathlon™ watches that are popular with runners. The price of these watches can vary from £20 to more than £100, depending on the brand and functions.

Sports watches with a lap function are useful for races, so that you can check your speed at each mile marker. They are also useful if you train on the track where you need to monitor carefully the speed of your efforts, and your recovery times between efforts. Some runners use a repeat 'countdown' function that enables them to programme their watch to bleep at regular intervals, to pace themselves while they are running (e.g. every 25 seconds if they are running 100 second laps) or to regulate their recovery times.

Heart rate monitors

The use of heart rate information in training is discussed in detail in chapter 10. Heart rate monitors can also be used to track your progress as you become fitter; to check for overtraining (by measuring your heart rate when you first wake up – see chapter 8), and to help you judge your pace. They are, however, expensive; and they are certainly not a necessary piece of equipment unless you choose to base your training on heart rate training zones.

Heart rate monitors consist of two components: a chest strap (sensor) and watch (receiver). The straps are interchangeable across the main models, and can be bought separately when you need them for around £30. The watch usually has the normal functions of a sports watch, as well as the heart rate functions.

Serious runners may want a heart rate monitor that can download stored data from the watch to a personal computer, using either a special interface unit or a microphone. This allows the runner to store and analyse the data from each session.

Some heart rate monitors estimate the number of calories expended in each workout, based on your gender and weight. This can help to provide additional motivation, although the calculations are not very accurate.

Pedometers and speed and distance monitors

Until recently, the only commercially available pedometers worked by counting the number of steps taken, and then multiplying by the average stride length (which was entered in advance). This approach is notoriously inaccurate, because your stride length depends on how fast you are going, how tired you are, and the terrain on which you are running. The estimates of the distance run therefore varied enormously.

In the last few years, new types of speed and distance monitors have become available which provide much more accurate estimates of the distance you run (and therefore your speed). These can work in one of two ways. The models from Nike™ and Fitsense™ include a small sensor that you tie into your shoelaces, which measures the acceleration of your feet and calculates your speed. The models from Timex™ include a receiver that you wear on your arm or belt that tracks its position using international navigation satellites. In both cases, the sensors transmit information about distance and speed to a watch worn on the wrist. This means that you can see your speed and distance in real time as you are running. The Fitsense™ watch also includes a heart rate monitor and records the data in a form that can be downloaded to a personal computer.[17]

Both methods seem to produce reasonably accurate results (within 1%), and can help you to train more effectively by providing information about the distance you have run and your speed. They are, however, quite expensive.

See chapter 2 for suggestions for other ways to measure the distances that you run.

Other kit

Apart from shoes, clothes and a watch, there is not much that a runner needs. However, you will find a range of useful items in your local specialist running shop. Some especially useful products are:

- a **wrist wallet**, or a small **shoe pocket** that interleaves in your shoelaces, to carry your door key or car key and some spare money for emergencies;
- a **bottle** for carrying water on long runs; this can be either a doughnut shaped bottle that goes round your hand (made by *Runners' Aid*) or a bottle that fits into a specially designed belt around your waist;
- a **reflective vest**, and wrist and ankle reflective straps, for running at night (you can get ankle straps with flashing lights on them in some bike shops);
- an **identity tag** to identify you in case of emergency, including any emergency medical information (e.g. allergies, blood group); you can either get this from a medical identity company such as MedicAlert, or you can do it yourself by getting a dog tag made (your local key-cutter can usually engrave one for you) with your name, phone number and any essential medical details;
- **plasters for blisters** – these are different from the normal plasters you get in chemists, as they are specifically designed to promote healing of blisters. You can put one of these over a blister and run immediately without noticing it at all. You can also use them to avoid blisters: I usually put on one before a marathon in the place where I would normally get a blister. Recommended brands of plaster specifically for blisters are *Compeed* and *Second Skin*;

- **Vaseline** (or another lubricant), which is used to prevent chafing in long runs; runners often apply copious quantities of Vaseline to the nipples, between the thighs, and under the arms towards the shoulder blades, all of which are areas that can rub. You can also buy special plasters designed to go over nipples to stop them from rubbing against your shirt or bra, though ordinary surgical tape or plasters do the job just as well.

Conclusion

Running is one of the cheapest sports to participate in. With the right pair of shoes and a sports bra you have all the equipment you need. But if you decide to run regularly all year round, it is a good idea to buy suitable clothes that will make you more comfortable.

My top tip is that I have a shoe wallet threaded through the laces of my running shoes, which contains a spare front door key, a £20 note, and a piece of paper with my name, address and medical details on it. This saves me having to remember, or having to carry, my keys and money when I go for a run.

The principles of running are basically the same for everyone, but there are some specific differences between men and women that affect running. This chapter looks at issues from the perspective of women runners, including biomechanical differences, the menstrual cycle, running during pregnancy, and issues of personal safety.

Biomechanical differences

As compared to men, women have wider hips and shoulders. Women are on average about 12 cm shorter and 18 kg lighter than men and they have about 8–10 per cent more body fat.[18] Women's legs are turned outwards more than men's, resulting in a greater misalignment of kneecap tracking, and women have a greater propensity to suffer from knee and hip injuries.

As a result, the prevalence of different types of running injuries varies between men and women, and the appropriate treatments are slightly different. On average, women suffer more than men from pain in the knee area. There is not much you need to do about this, apart from follow good advice to avoid injury and ensure that any medical advice you get is from a properly qualified and experienced practitioner.

Because of these biomechanical differences, women's running shoes ought to be designed to be rather different from men's (for example, they should have greater control to prevent overpronation). There are running shoes made especially for women, but studies have found that they don't make much difference.[19] They are generally more comfortable, however, because they are designed for narrower feet.

Running and periods

The impact of periods on your running performance

It is not clear whether exercise performance changes much during the menstrual cycle. Individual women appear to respond in different ways, and many women show no effect at all.

On the whole, unless you are sure that your period affects your running, there is no strong reason to adjust your running around your menstrual cycle. However, if you are an endurance athlete, and you suffer from water retention and weight gain at certain times during your cycle, this may reduce your performance at particular times of the month.

It is worth keeping track of your menstrual cycle in your training log (see chapter 2), in case you are one of those runners whose performance is affected by your menstrual cycle. (This information will also help you to rule out this possible explanation of a poor performance in the future.) If your performance is related to your periods, then a complete training log will help you to identify the times of the month when you are likely to be affected by your cycle.

The impact of running on your periods

Many women runners find that exercise can improve their mood and reduce discomfort before and during their periods. Moderate exercise can relieve the physical symptoms of premenstrual tension, including tender breasts.

In some runners, particularly those who are training for long distances, running can lead to *amenorrhea* – that is, erratic or absent periods. The reasons for exercise-induced amenorrhea are not well understood. It seems to be caused by some combination of low body fat, inadequate nutrition and stress. Young runners who train intensively seem to be especially prone to menstrual irregularity.[20]

Amenorrhea induced by exercise is generally temporary, and periods return when the training load is reduced. It may, however, have a long-term negative impact because it increases the chances of osteoporosis. as a result of low levels of oestrogen, a hormone that helps to protect calcium in bones. There is also evidence of lower bone density in women who miss their periods; and this can lead to increased risk of stress fractures and brittle bones later in life. Amenorrhea is also associated with increased risk of cancer of the uterus and breast.

If you suffer from irregularities in your periods, you should see a gynaecologist, both to rule out other, more serious, causes, and to try to identify steps that you can take to restore your normal cycle. You should look carefully at your diet, to ensure that you are getting enough calcium, protein and fat (see below). You should also consider whether you are suffering from other symptoms of overtraining, such as elevated heart rate, insomnia or fluctuating weight (see chapter 8). Persistent amenorrhea can be treated with hormone therapy.

Running and pregnancy

Most doctors now agree that moderate exercise during pregnancy is good for both mother and baby. There is evidence that women who exercise before and during pregnancy have less complicated pregnancies and births.[21]

However, you should not continue to run during pregnancy as if nothing has changed. Your body does change with pregnancy, and this means that some activities that are safe when you are not pregnant are not safe for you or your baby when you are pregnant. For example, ligaments and bones soften during pregnancy, to accommodate the baby, which means that you are more susceptible to injury. Your temperature regulation mechanisms are strained, which means it is easier to overheat, which could damage the foetus, especially in the early stages of pregnancy. You should avoid intensive exercise with high heart rates (e.g. above 140 beats per minute – see chapter 10) to avoid depriving your body of oxygen.

You should check with your doctor before running while pregnant, both to discuss general guidelines, and to check that you don't present any particular risk factors that indicate that you should not run while pregnant (such as hypertension, premature dilation of the cervix, and persistent bleeding).

'I kept running until six weeks before my daughter was born. Just run how you feel, and listen to both your bodies. I started running again a week after Emily was born. Fortunately, she loves endorphins in her milk!'

Swenja Surminski, London

If you do decide to continue to run, here are some guidelines:

- don't run to **exhaustion**; and don't run at high levels of intensity (e.g. sprinting) which may affect the baby's oxygen supply;
- be careful not to **overheat**, especially during the early weeks;
- be careful not to **dehydrate**, which entails that you may need to drink more than you are used to;
- maintain your **blood sugar levels**, which entails you should **eat** more than you are used to;
- don't try to stick to a **training schedule**, or try to maintain your previous heart rate zones; instead, run as you feel inclined and listen to your (and your baby's) body; you might want to use a heart rate monitor to ensure that you don't elevate your heart rate too much;
- when running **no longer feels comfortable**, consider other exercise, such as swimming or aqua-jogging, to keep fit. An exercise bike will help you to keep fit, and may be useful later on if you are at home alone with the baby.

If you develop any of the following symptoms, you should stop running immediately and consult a doctor:

- bloody discharge or amniotic fluid leakage from the vagina;
- sudden swelling of the ankles, hands or face;
- persistent, severe headaches or visual disturbance;
- swelling, pain and redness of the calf in one leg;
- elevation of pulse rate or blood pressure that persists after exercise;

The Race for Life 5 km

- excessive fatigue or any palpitations or chest pains;
- persistent contractions (they may suggest the onset of premature labour);
- unexplained abdominal pain;
- insufficient weight gain.

Breastfeeding

If you decide to breastfeed your baby, monitor the baby's weight gain carefully. If the baby does not appear to be putting on weight as quickly as expected, this could be because running is reducing the amount of milk you produce, and you may need to cut back on exercise.

It is usually more comfortable for your breasts if you run after rather than before a feed. You can, however, safely breastfeed as soon as you like after running. You should be aware that immediately after exercise your breast milk may contain lactic acid. This will not harm your baby, but some babies don't like it. You may need to wait for an hour after your run for the lactic acid level to return to normal.

Nutrition for women runners

We shall look at a balanced diet for runners in chapter 6. However, there are a few issues that affect women more than men.

First, you should ensure that you get enough **iron** in your diet. Iron is essential for transporting oxygen through your bloodstream, as well as providing a key building block of muscle tissue. It is easy for women to become anaemic (i.e. have insufficient iron) because of menstruation. In addition, some women don't eat red meat, which is a major dietary source of iron. If you don't eat red meat, make sure that you get iron from sources such as dark green vegetables, beans and dried fruit. Avoid drinking coffee or tea with your meals, as these interfere with the absorption of iron. Watch carefully for the symptoms of anaemia, which include fatigue, palpitations, dizziness, dryness of mouth, sores in the corner of the mouth and brittle hair. Your doctor can easily test for iron deficiency. If necessary take a food supplement to maintain your iron levels.

Second, you should ensure that you have enough **calcium**. This is essential for building strong bones, and avoiding osteoporosis; it may also help to reduce high blood pressure. Dairy products are generally a good source of calcium; if you don't eat dairy products then try to buy calcium-fortified alternatives (you can buy calcium-fortified mineral water, orange juice and soya milk, for example).

Third, some women runners don't eat enough **fat**. You need some fat in your diet, not least to ensure that you have healthy hair and skin. Remember that some fats are good for you – try to increase your intake of monounsaturated fats (e.g. from olive oil and nuts) and essential fatty acids (e.g. from oily fish and seeds) while avoiding saturated fats (which mainly come from animal products). See chapter 6 for more details. Insufficient fat is highly correlated with amenorrhea (i.e. irregular periods – see above), which can have long term health repercussions.

Eating disorders

The number of women suffering from anorexia nervosa and bulimia nervosa is growing in many Western societies. People with *anorexia nervosa* restrict their food intake and have a distorted image of their bodies. A person with *bulimia nervosa* may also restrict food intake, but binges occasionally, usually following this with self-induced vomiting or the use of laxatives. On the negative side, compulsive running can be a symptom of an eating disorder. On the positive side, running can improve your self-image and help to control body weight without resort to unhealthy eating habits.

Running as a symptom of eating disorders

Compulsive exercising, including running, can be a symptom of bulimia. Running can be a popular sport for women on the margin of bulimia, because it is such an effective way of burning calories.

It is sometimes difficult to recognise the early symptoms of eating disorders, especially in yourself. It is important for people close to us – particularly family and good friends – to pay attention. While it is normal for competitive athletes to pay attention to their weight, some women runners may become fixated on their body weight. If you suspect that you, or someone close to you, may be suffering from an eating disorder, **you should seek expert help right away**. Anorexia and bulimia are serious illnesses, and can be very damaging and, in extreme cases, fatal.

There is a larger group of people who don't suffer from an eating disorder but who are a little bit too obsessive about what they eat. They sometimes live under a tyranny of counting every calorie, or every gram of fat. This can be stressful for them, and those around them, and can be unhealthy if they are too restrictive in what they eat because they don't get a balanced diet containing all the nutrients, vitamins and minerals that they need. It is also frequently self-defeating: all too often they will go hungry throughout the day, eating too little for breakfast and lunch, and are so

---

A runner's journey from an eating disorder

'It has been a journey of sorts over the course of nearly nine years. Something like a long, hard cross-country course: undulating, rough ground, changeable weather – sometimes for and sometimes against!

What started out as a very negative and destructive relationship between food and running turned a corner and developed into a solid working partnership. Running alone helped me to gain self-reliance, strength and self-confidence. Little by little I learned that to build on these traits required nourishment, both physically and emotionally, and that running tended to both these needs. Whereas running used to be a weapon used against food, slowly and gently it became an ally. Fuelling-up appropriately and pushing myself to finish a hard run, knowing and trusting that my body will carry me through to a strong finish instead of ending a race with feelings of emptiness and weakness is truly an empowering feeling. It's given me the sense that, through effort, sheer hard work and respect for both others and myself, anything is possible!'

Nia Parry, 28, London

hungry by the end of the day that they eat too much. As we shall see in chapter 6, it is healthier to eat a large breakfast, and to eat little and often throughout the day.

Running as a way to a positive self-image

In chapter 6 we shall look at how we can use exercise to help to manage weight and body fat. In general, exercise is a much less damaging, and more sustainable, way to lose weight than dieting. Controlling what you eat can be negative, destructive and unhealthy; while managing your weight through exercise promotes a positive self-image, confidence, and a healthy, sustainable lifestyle.

Personal safety

There are a number of steps that women can take to minimise the risks to their personal safety while running.

The best bet is to try to **avoid running on your own in the dark**. If possible, run with a friend, join a local running club, or arrange to run in daylight. This will ensure that you have a more relaxing workout than if you are on edge and on your own.

Other steps you can take include:

- carry a **mobile phone**, so that you can call for help if you need it; you can also carry an inexpensive rape alarm (mace and pepper sprays are not legal in the UK);
- avoid **remote and unlit areas**, and keep away from trees and bushes;
- **vary your routine**, so that you don't always run the same route at a predictable time;
- avoid using **headphones** while running; listening to music makes it more difficult to hear strangers coming up behind you (as well as making you more vulnerable to cars, dogs, roller-bladers, etc);
- make sure **someone knows where you are going** and when you are expected back; make sure they know what to do if you don't return in good time;
- don't wear **expensive jewellery** that might attract unwelcome attention.

Conclusion

More and more women are taking up running. For example, about half the members of my running club are women. Running empowers and liberates us all, giving us space to change our perspective.

One of the most common challenges faced by women runners is that of irregular or missed periods, a condition that is normal from time to time but can lead to long-term health problems if it persists. It can be avoided provided you look after yourself and eat well.

You are never too young, or too old, to be a runner. But there are some special considerations you should take into account, depending on your circumstances.

Young people

Exercise is generally good for young people, and in Britain today they are increasingly doing too little of it. That is one reason why levels of obesity are rising among young people, storing up significant health problems for themselves, and for society, in the future. As well as gaining improved health, young people who exercise are more likely to do well at school and have more self-confidence and a better body image. Girls who run are less likely to suffer from negative images of their bodies; and are less likely to be come pregnant as teenagers.[22]

Running is an excellent sport for young people, requiring little investment or special skills. It is infinitely flexible, allowing young runners to do as little or as much as they want.

Do you need to start young?

Some sports – such as tennis and swimming – seem to need training from a young age in order to reach world-class status. This is not the case with endurance sports such as running. There is no evidence to suggest that there are physiological benefits to training as children that cannot be obtained by training after the age of 18. Indeed, the opposite is true: children who do well at school often don't go on to perform competitively as adults. One explanation for this is that runners appear to have a finite period of time during which they can compete. If young people compete intensively, they may expend their competitive years by the time they are 20, and so lose the opportunity to compete when they are at their physical and mental peak. It may also be that young people who are pushed into running by a parent or teacher give up the sport as soon as they are able to assert control of their lives.

How to avoid doing too much exercise

Young people are usually good judges of how much running they should be doing. Generally, for people under 18, the best advice is to do what you enjoy, and not to train too intensively.

Parents who are themselves keen runners, or who have ambitions for their children, should be careful not to push them too far and too fast. Create the opportunities for your child, but don't put too much pressure on him or her.

As a rule of thumb, children should not train for middle distance races (e.g. 800 m and 1500 m) until they are about 13 or 14; and longer races (e.g. 10 km) should be put on hold until the young person is 16.

Running injuries occur in young runners as they do for all runners, especially when training levels are increased too fast. Like all runners, young runners should ensure that they don't increase their mileage too rapidly. This can be a particular problem for runners who train mainly at school or at college, if they resume training after a long summer holiday during which they have not run much.

The requirements of young runners

For young people who run occasionally, there is no need to buy specialist running shoes. But if they run more than 10 miles a week, then you should buy appropriate running shoes from a specialist running store.

There are no specific dietary considerations for children who run: they need basically the same diet as any other child. While they should certainly not be eating a diet of high-fat, highly processed food, they should not be prevented from eating foods that are appropriate to growing bodies, including more calories and lots of protein and calcium. Because protein and calcium often come from foods that are

---

Ten guidelines for parents of children in sports

1. Make sure your children know that – win or lose – you love them and are not disappointed with their performance.
2. Be realistic about your child's physical ability.
3. Help your child set realistic goals.
4. Emphasise improved performance, not winning. Positively reinforce improved skills.
5. Don't relive your own athletic past through your child.
6. Provide a safe environment for training and competition.
7. Control your own emotions at games and events. Don't yell at other players, coaches, or officials.
8. Be a cheerleader for your child and the other children on the team.
9. Respect your child's coaches. Communicate openly with them. If you disagree with their approach, discuss it with them.
10. Be a positive role model. Enjoy sports yourself. Set your own goals. Live a healthy lifestyle.

The Physician and Sportsmedicine (1988).

relatively high in fat, an appropriate diet for a young person may well have more calories and more fats than a health-conscious adult would eat.

Children are at greater risk of overheating than adults, because their ratio of body mass to surface area is lower, they sweat less and they produce more heat. So it is important to make sure that young runners drink enough to keep their body temperatures low. Chapter 6 contains more information about dehydration.

Veteran runners

Running is an excellent sport for people as they get older. As we shall see, it provides significant benefits that can offset the effects of ageing. Some people take up running so that they can keep fit and trim when they no longer feel able to participate in contact sports such as football and rugby. (More than half the runners in the New York City Marathon are over 40.)

The effects of ageing

From the thirties onwards, a number of physical changes take place in the average person's body. Aerobic capacity decreases, muscle mass reduces, muscle elasticity reduces, lung elasticity declines, bone density reduces, the metabolism slows, body fat increases and the immune system becomes weaker.

These changes will have an adverse impact on running performance. The fall in aerobic capacity, reduced stride length, reduced leg strength, and reduced ability to

Bob Davidson, looking good at 70 years young

store energy all contribute to a deterioration in performance. In general, it is thought that running speeds over any distance deteriorate by about 1 per cent a year from a peak at some point in the thirties; and we appear to lose aerobic capacity at about 9–10 per cent a decade.

However, older runners can continue to perform extraordinary athletic feats. Canadian athlete Ed Whitlock ran a marathon in 3:00:24 in 2001, at the age of 70. Carlos Lopes set the world marathon record at the age of 38. Hal Higdon, marathon runner and writer, at the age of 52 ran a 10 km in 31:08 and a marathon in 2:29:27.

The benefits of running for older people

The health benefits of running are broadly the same for older people as for everybody else. They include reductions in the risks of heart disease, diabetes, high blood pressure and

41

> 'Age brings problems; it also brings solutions. For every disadvantage there is an advantage. For every measurable loss there is an immeasurable gain.'
>
> *George Sheehan, Personal Best, 1989*

cancer; reduced depression and anxiety; weight control; improved bones, muscles and joints; improved mobility and co-ordination, and a psychological sense of well-being. What is especially significant for older people is that the risk of developing these conditions grows as you get older, so the benefits of running are increased. It is especially beneficial for older people that running can improve muscle strength, co-ordination and bone density, all reducing the risk of falling and fracturing bones, and so increasing the prospects for living independently.[23]

Age categories

One of the reasons for the running boom in the last twenty years has been the growing use of age categories and prizes in many running events, which has enabled older runners to compete in races and have the opportunity to compare themselves with others in their age groups.

In the UK, the main age categories are shown in table 5.1.

Age grading

Another way to adjust athletes' performances with age has come with the introduction of age-grading tables. These were developed by the World Association of Veteran Athletes, the world governing body for track and field, long-distance running and race walking for veteran athletes. The tables were first published in 1989.

The tables work by recording the world record performance for each age (interpolated where necessary) at each distance, for men and women. For example, the world record for a 53-year-old woman running a 10 km is 35:01. So if a 53-year-old woman finishes a 10 km in 45:18, she has an age-graded performance of 77.3 per cent (which is 35:01 divided by 45:18).

The wide availability of age-grading tables has allowed older runners to compete on even terms with younger generations. In many running clubs today, the age-graded champion earns as much, if not more, recognition as the outright (non-age adjusted) winner of the event.

Table 5.1 Main age categories

	Men	Women
Under 20	Under 20	Under 20
Seniors	20–39	20–35
Veteran	40–49	35–49
V50	50–59	50–59
V60	60–69	60–69

Age grading can be used to compare performances across different ages and sexes; track your own performance over time; identify your best events; set goals for current and future years; and identify your best ever performance.

How to start running as an older person

There is no such thing as someone who is too old to start running. Running helps to slow down the effects of ageing, improves the health, fitness and mobility of older people, and improves psychological health.

Anyone over the age of 50 should get a check-up by a doctor before they begin any programme of physical exercise (see chapter 2 for other indications of when it is necessary to get an all-clear from a doctor). In older people, the doctor will be particularly checking for heart disease, diabetes and high blood pressure, to ensure that they can run safely.

Apart from getting a check-up from a doctor, the advice for a new older runner is basically the same as for everyone else, and set out in detail in chapter 2. The main priorities are to build up slowly, and set yourself demanding but achievable goals.

Tips for older runners

The decline in performance with age is not preordained. For example, the rate of decline of aerobic capacity can be halved to about 5 per cent a decade, or even less, with the right training.

Here are some ways to manage the effects of ageing:

- **cut back the mileage**, but increase your training quality (there is nothing to stop you from continuing to do fast speed work on the track – this is how Hal Higdon has continued his remarkable performances);
- take **more rest days** between sessions, and avoid overtraining;
- increase the **variety of your aerobic training**, for example by aqua-running, cycling, swimming, and skiing;
- **warm up** carefully before running, and **stretch afterwards**, to protect muscles, which are less elastic and more prone to injury than they were when you were younger;
- increase your **weight training**, to compensate for the decline in muscle mass that you would otherwise experience.

Conclusion

My running club has members aged from 17 to over 80 years old. Remarkably, because we share a common interest, there are strong friendships across the years. We have formed deep and lasting relationships that enrich all our lives. Running transcends all ages. For young people, it is a gateway to sports of all kinds. It is an affordable, accessible and safe way to embark on a life of healthy exercise.

There is nothing inevitable about the deterioration in performance that comes as we get older. With smart training, you can offset or reverse the effects of ageing, and continue to grow and improve as a runner. Some of my running friends are forty years older than me – and still running marathons. I hope that I too will have the courage, wisdom and good fortune to go on enjoying running as long as I'm still breathing.

As we get older, running helps to reduce the impact of age on our fitness, strength, mobility and independence. It can thereby give us many extra years of good quality of life. George Sheehan, the philosopher of running, wrote this a few years before he died:

'The unfit youth or young adult or even middle aged person can still be independent and enjoy life. The ageing cannot. The normal loss of physical powers that occurs with inactivity makes fitness a necessity. . . .

In time, regardless of how we play, we will all depart. What we must avoid is having our actual leaving precede that departure – to die in effect before we die in truth, to live out our years in a joyless, dependent existence, our body and mind and soul already waiting for us on the other side of the divide.'

One of the pleasures of being a runner is that you can eat and drink considerably more than if you have a sedentary lifestyle, and still feel healthy and avoid putting on weight. Running enables you to escape from the constant hunger, self-denial and self-loathing of dieting, and instead enables you to eat a wide variety of foods more or less as you please.

Nutrition is the third most important determinant of your running performance, after genetics and training. If you want to be a good runner, you have to eat and drink the right things. This chapter is about the food and drink you need to maintain a healthy body; the next chapter is about how you should eat and drink before, during and after running.

> 'Some people eat to run. Others run to eat.'
>
> *Phil, club runner, 44*

The main rule for a balanced diet for a typical healthy adult is to **eat from a wide range of unprocessed foods**. If you do this, you will not go far wrong. There are several good books about nutrition for athletes that you should read if you want more detail, or if you have special needs (for example, if you are vegetarian or allergic to particular foods).[24] This chapter introduces the key principles for runners.

The main nutrients

The main nutrients for human beings are carbohydrates, fats, protein and water.

Carbohydrates

Carbohydrates are mainly used for energy. Foods that are high in carbohydrate include potatoes, pasta, rice, bread, fruit, cereals, pulses and anything sugary.

Carbohydrates vary in the complexity of their chemical structure, which in turn affects how quickly they are absorbed into the bloodstream. Scientists have developed the *Glycaemic Index* (GI), which ranks foods according to their immediate effect on blood sugar levels. For example, apples have a GI of 38, which means that eating an apple gives about 38 per cent of the increase in blood sugar that would be gained from eating pure glucose.

Table 6.1 Examples of high, medium and low glycaemic index foods

High GI foods		Moderate GI foods		Low GI foods	
Food	GI	Food	GI	Food	GI
Glucose	100	All Bran™	42	Chick peas	33
Cornflakes	84	Muesli	56	Green lentils	30
Weetabix	69	Buckwheat	54	Red lentils	26
Brown rice	76	Basmati rice	58	Soya beans	18
White rice	87	Spaghetti	41	Kidney beans	27
Bagel	72	Muffin	44	Apples	38
Baguette	95	Carrots	49	Pears	38
Parsnip	97	Peas	48	Plums	39
Baked potato	85	Baked beans	48	Peanuts	14
Raisins	64	Banana	55	Milk	27
Mars bar	68	Orange	44	Yoghurt	33

The glycaemic index was originally developed to help diabetics to manage their blood sugar, but it is becoming more widely recognised as a tool for healthy eating. You will need to look at the GI of the meal as a whole (which you can estimate by a weighted average of the GI of the main components).

Generally, you should eat low-GI meals, because these don't lead to such large variations in your blood sugar and insulin levels. Big swings in your blood sugar can lead to higher levels of body fat, reduced immunity from infection, mood swings and stress, and impaired storage of energy by muscles.

However, high GI foods are very useful when you need energy quickly, such as immediately before, during and after exercise (see chapter 7).

Fats

Fats are found in oily food, especially animal products, and food cooked in oils. Fats vary in their chemical structure, which in turn makes a difference to how they are handled by the human body and their impact on health. Some fats are harmful, and some are essential for health. Table 6.2 summarises the main categories.

In general, many people in Western societies eat more fat than they should; and too much of it is harmful saturated fats. You should be getting around 15–25 per cent of your daily calories from fat, instead of an average of over 40 per cent in Britain. But you should not try to cut fats out of your diet altogether. Try to get most of your fats from monounsaturated fats, such as olive oil, nuts and avocados; and ensure that you have sufficient essential fatty acids, which you get from oily fish and seeds.

Protein

Proteins are the building blocks of the human body. About 20 per cent of your body weight is protein. It is mainly needed for growth and repair of body tissues, though it can also be used as fuel for energy. It plays an important role in the health of your blood system.

The protein you eat is broken down into amino acids, and then recombined to make suitable human proteins. There are 20 amino acids, of which 12 can be

Table 6.2 Types of fat and their health implications

Type of fat	Health implications	Sources
Saturated	Heart disease, increase in cholesterol.	Butter, lard, cheese, animal fats. Biscuits, cakes, pastry. Palm oil and coconut oil.
Monounsaturated	Good for you. Can reduce harmful cholesterol.	Olive, rapeseed, groundnut, hazelnut, almond oils. Avocados, olives, nuts, seeds.
Polyunsaturated	Can reduce both good and harmful cholesterol.	Most vegetable oils and oily fish.
The following fatty acids are specific types of polyunsaturated fat:		
Omega 3 essential fatty acids	Health of blood and blood vessels. Reduced heart disease, lower blood pressure.	Oily fish (e.g. mackerel, fresh tuna, salmon, sardines). Linseed (flax), pumpkin seeds, walnuts, rapeseed oil, soyabeans.
Omega 6 essential fatty acids	Health of cell membranes. (But can reduce good cholesterol; high intake may be cancer risk.)	Vegetable oils, polyunsaturated margarine.

manufactured in the body; but eight of them, called 'essential amino acids', cannot, and they must be obtained from what you eat.

Some foods contain all eight essential amino acids – these include dairy products, eggs, meat and fish. Other foods such as cereals, pulses and nuts have some, but not all, of the essential amino acids and must be eaten in the right combinations to ensure the body has all the components it needs. Vegetarians, and anyone else who does not eat much meat, should ensure that they combine foods from two or more of the following four categories:

- **pulses** (beans, lentils, peas)
- **grains** (bread, pasta, rice, cereals, corn, rye)
- **nuts and seeds** (peanuts, sunflower seeds, pumpkin seeds)
- **quorn, tofu** and **soya products** (soya milk, tofu, tempeh, etc.)

For example, baked beans on toast is an excellent combination that provides all the essential amino acids.

If you exercise regularly, and especially if you do strength training, you need much more protein than if you are sedentary, to enable you to rebuild and repair muscles. The current recommended daily intake of protein for a sedentary person is 0.75 g of protein a day for every kilogram of body weight; whereas people who exercise need 1.25–1.75 g of protein a day for every kilogram of body weight.[25]

Table 6.3 Protein allowance

Lifestyle	Grammes per day/per kg	Example for 60 kg person	Example for 80 kg person
Sedentary	0.75	45 g/day	60 g/day
Endurance runner	1.3	78 g/day	104 g/day
Strength athlete	1.6	96 g/day	128 g/day

You can safely eat more protein than this calculation implies, but once your body has used the protein it needs, the extra protein will be burned as energy.

Eating a balanced diet

Your energy intake should come from a mixture of carbohydrates, fats and protein, made up roughly as follows:

- 15–25% of calories from fat;
- 60–70% of calories from carbohydrates;
- 15–25% of calories from protein.

From these broad proportions, an estimate of your overall energy requirements (see below) and the amount of protein you need, you can estimate the amount of carbohydrate, fat and protein you should have in your diet. However, you should be aware of the fact that the different types of food provide different amounts of energy for each gram (see table 6.4).

Table 6.4 Energy from different nutrients

Energy source	Energy (kcal)
1 g of carbohydrate	4
1 g of fat	9
1 g of protein	4

Because fat has more than twice as many calories per gram as carbohydrates and protein, you should eat a lower proportion of fat *by weight of food* than the proportion of fat measured by *calories provided*. So if fat is 20 per cent of your diet by calories, it should only be 10 per cent of your diet by weight.

Within this basic structure of your nutrient intake, try to eat at least five portions of fruit and vegetables a day (a portion is about 80 g – equivalent to an apple or two tomatoes).

Later in this chapter, we shall look at the way you can adjust this calculation if you want to lose weight.

Table 6.5 Sample breakdown of carbohydrate, fat and protein

Nutrient	2500 Kilocalories a day		3500 Kilocalories a day	
	Calories	Grams	Calories	Grams
Carbohydrate	1500 kcal 60%	375 g 68%	2100 kcal 60%	525 g 68%
Fat	500 kcal 20%	56 g 10%	700 kcal 20%	78 g 10%
Protein	500 kcal 20%	125 g 22%	700 kcal 20%	175 g 22%

Calculating your daily calorie requirement

To calculate the number of calories you need to consume each day, you should calculate your normal energy needs (which depends on your age and weight), adjust for your metabolic rate (which depends on how active you are) and add the calories you burn exercising (which depends on what exercise you do).[26] This is easier than it sounds at first, and the calculation is set out below. Alternatively, you can feed your personal information into a calculator on the internet (see, for example, the calculators at <www.serpentine.org.uk/software>).

The **first step** is to estimate your resting calorie requirement. Simply enter your weight (in kilograms) into one of the formulas in table 6.6.

Table 6.6 Resting metabolic requirement[27]

Age	Men	Women
10–18 years	$17.5 \times W + 651$	$12.2 \times W + 746$
19–30 years	$15.3 \times W + 679$	$14.7 \times W + 496$
31–60 years	$11.6 \times W + 879$	$8.7 \times W + 829$

Example: I weigh 74 kg, and I am a 35-year-old male, so my resting metabolic requirement is: $(11.6 \times 74) + 879 = 1737$ *calories per day*.

The **second step** is to multiply this by your activity level:

Table 6.7 Activity level and metabolic rates

Activity level	Multiplier
Sedentary	1.4
Moderately active (e.g. regularly walking during the day)	1.7
Very active	2.0

Example: I am moderately active, because I have a sedentary job as a civil servant, but I exercise every day, including cycling to work and running. So I multiply by 1.7: *1.7 × 1737 = 2953 calories per day*.

Finally, the **third step** is to add the number of calories you expend on average each day exercising. If you run, you can estimate this as 100 calories for every mile you run.

Example: Because I run about 40–45 miles a week, which is an average of about 6 miles a day, I add 600 calories: *2953 + 600 = 3553 calories a day.*

My equilibrium energy intake should consequently be around 3553 calories a day. (This means that, luckily, I can eat pretty much anything I want.)

In reality, there is considerable variation from person to person. Some people are born with a higher metabolic rate than others. If you have a large amount of lean muscle tissue you will tend to burn more energy than someone who does not. So you cannot use this calculation as a hard-and-fast rule. Instead, use it as a rule of thumb to get an idea of the sort of calorie intake you are likely to need, and then see what works for you in practice.

Table 6.8 Calories expended in typical exercises[28]

Activity	Kcal/hour
Aerobics (high intensity)	520
Aerobics (low intensity)	400
Cycling (16 km/hour)	385
Cycling (9 km/hour)	250
Running (6 min/mile)	1000
Running (10 min/mile)	600
Squash	615
Swimming (vigorous)	630
Weight training	270–450

Note: This table assumes a person weighing 65 kg. Calorie consumption would be higher for heavier people.

Vitamins and minerals

Vitamins and minerals are not a source of energy, but they are needed by the body to maintain your health. Inadequate vitamins or minerals can certainly have a harmful impact on your running performance. However, if you eat a balanced diet of largely unprocessed foods, it is likely that you are getting enough of the key vitamins and minerals.

In judging your vitamin and mineral intake you should take the following into account:

- if you are eating **packaged or processed** foods, they may have fewer vitamins and minerals than fresh food;
- intensive **food production** (e.g. farming, storage and transportation) means that some foods don't have as many minerals and vitamins as their less intensively produced counterparts;

- if you **sweat** a lot (e.g. because you are running in a hot climate) you may lose essential minerals in your sweat, which need to be replaced;
- regular **exercise increases your vitamin and mineral requirements** compared with sedentary people, because they are needed for metabolism, maintenance of tissue and manufacture of red blood cells; the recommended daily allowances (RDAs) that are published by the Government are a guide for the general population, and you may well need to consume more than these guidelines;
- high-intensity training may **weaken your immune system**, and increased intakes of vitamin C will help to boost your natural defences;
- it is possible to **take too much of some vitamins and minerals** (particularly vitamins that are not water soluble, such Vitamins A, B_6 and D); large excesses of these can lead to nutritional imbalance and, in extreme cases, serious illness.

On the whole, you should aim to get your vitamin and mineral intake from your diet. However, many active people choose to supplement their diet by taking a **multivitamin supplement**. This provides insurance, in case the vitamins are lacking from the food you eat. But you should not take doses of vitamins or minerals significantly above the recommended daily allowance without first seeking medical advice.

Water

Water is by far the most important nutrient in the runner's diet. Yet for some reason it is often neglected in books and articles about running.

You should almost certainly drink more water than you do right now. This is for two reasons. First, most people – even if they don't do any exercise – don't drink enough water. Second, as a runner you need more water because you lose water through sweat.

Water is important because it helps to regulate your body temperature (through sweating), and it makes up 82 per cent of blood and determines its viscosity. Water is also stored with glycogen in your muscles, so if you don't drink enough water your body will not be able to store energy. High water intake will also help your body to regulate toxins, and keep your skin healthy. As we shall see in chapter 7, dehydration rapidly results in poor performance.

Drinking water

As a rule of thumb, you need about 1 litre of water for every 1000 kcal you consume during the day (this is your base water intake; you need extra when you are exercising). You also need more in hot or humid weather. This means that if you have a daily calorie intake of 3000 kcal, you need to drink about 3 litres of water each day. That is a lot, and may well be more than you are drinking at the moment.

Try to get into the habit of drinking a pint of water when you first get out of bed; and then sip water throughout the day. Many healthy people keep a sports water bottle next to them at work, so that they can sip frequently.

The following drinks are diuretics – that is, they make you urinate and so increase the amount of water you need:

- Coffee and tea
- Caffeinated drinks such as cola or Red Bull™
- Alcoholic drinks

If you drink any of these, you should aim to increase your water intake by at least the volume of the diuretic drink. (So if you have a 350 ml can of cola, try to drink 350 ml extra of water as well.)

The urine colour test

It is fairly straightforward to check if you are drinking enough, by looking at the colour of your urine. If your urine is clear, then you are well hydrated. If it is yellow, or dark, then you are dehydrated and need to drink more. (The University of Connecticut has developed a guide, like a paint colour chart, to enable you to judge your hydration!) Note that your urine may be discoloured by some vitamins and minerals – for example, Vitamin B_6 tends to make your urine fluorescent yellow – so that if you take vitamin supplements you may not be able to judge your hydration so easily by looking at the colour.

Rapid weight loss is also a good indicator of dehydration. If you weigh yourself after a workout and find you have lost a lot of weight, then you should not congratulate yourself, but go to the kitchen and get yourself a pint of water or sports drink.

What is your ideal weight?

We know that there are disadvantages in being overweight, including strong correlations between obesity and various forms of heart disease and cancer. But there are also good reasons to avoid being too thin. Low body weight and low body fat will make you ill. The link is especially strong in women, for whom low body fat is associated with irregular periods, brittle bones and reduced fertility (see chapter 4). Reducing your food intake to levels that make you underweight will deprive you of essential nutrients. If you have too little body fat, your body will break down muscle and other essential tissues, which is unhealthy as well as damaging to your running performance. So the trick is to find an equilibrium weight that keeps you trim and healthy, and without making you too thin.

There are two basic ways to estimate whether you need to lose weight. The simplest is to see whether you weigh too much for your height. The more complicated approach is to estimate how much of your total weight is accounted for by body fat. These approaches are explained below. But everybody (and every body) is different, so there are no hard and fast rules.

Body mass index (BMI)

The most common way to think about whether you are overweight is to look at your *body mass index* (BMI). This is calculated by comparing your weight with your height, using the following formula:

BMI = weight in kilograms/(height in metres)²

Example: I weigh 74 kg and my height is 1.87 m, so my BMI is $74/(1.87)^2 = 21.2$.

Table 6.9 sets out the average assessments of your BMI measurement.

However the BMI scale, and other similar methods based on comparing weight and height, are fairly crude and should be treated with caution. You may weigh a lot for your height because you have excess fat (which might be a problem). But you may

Table 6.9 Body Mass Index assessment

BMI	Assessment
18.5 or less	Underweight
18.5–24.9	Normal
25.0–29.9	Overweight
30.0–34.9	Obese
35.0–39.9	Very obese
40 or greater	Extremely obese

have a high BMI because you are a stocky build, or because you work out in the gym and have more than average lean muscle tissue. Also, this BMI scale is only suitable for adults aged 20–65 and it may not be appropriate for all ethnic groups.

Percentage body fat

In addition to comparing your weight with your height, you can also look at your percentage body fat. To measure this accurately requires full submersion in a tank of liquid, which isn't practical for most of us! However, your body fat can be approximated in a number of other ways, including measuring the ratio of your waist to your hips, using callipers to measure your near-surface body fat, or using equipment which estimates your fat by measuring your electrical resistance.

For example, you can buy bathroom scales (made by Tanita™) that estimate your body fat by measuring your electrical resistance. These work best for tracking changes in body fat if you measure yourself at the same time of day. However, this form of measurement can be significantly distorted by your level of hydration, and the calculation depends on assumptions about a range of other factors such as the amount of lean muscle in your body.

Once you have got an estimate of your percentage body fat, what does it mean? According to the American Council on Exercise, body fat levels of greater than 25 per cent for men, and 31 per cent for women indicate clinical obesity.

Table 6.10 Implications of percentage body fat

	Women	Men
Minimum level of fat required	10–12%	2–4%
Athletes	14–20%	6–13%
Fit	21–24%	14–17%
Acceptable	25–31%	18–25%
Obese	32% plus	25% plus

Losing weight

Lots of us start running because we want to lose weight. Some competitive runners want to lose weight in order to increase their performance. This section is about the principles of weight loss for runners.

Obesity is a growing problem in Britain, with around half of women and two-thirds of men currently overweight or obese. This can lead to poor health, including heart disease and diabetes, and reduced life expectancy. It also reduces quality of life, both physically and psychologically.

> 'For me, running is a means of getting slim in a happy atmosphere.'
>
> *James Stratford*

Many of us find that running is a good way to escape this disease. Runners benefit from a virtuous circle of weight loss, increased self-esteem, improved performance and commitment to a healthier lifestyle.

Running is an ideal way of losing fat and improving your appearance. It increases your energy consumption, allowing you to continue to eat satisfying amounts of food while reducing your levels of body fat. Conversely, weight loss is an effective way to improve your running. For competitive athletes, reaching the correct body weight is an important component in improving performance. However, if you reduce your weight and body fat too much, you can make yourself ill, and your performance will deteriorate.

Why running is a good way to lose weight

In my view, diets are not a good way to lose weight because:

- many people on diets are **perpetually hungry**; and although they may reduce their food intake for a time, it is unlikely that they will be able to maintain their lower weight;
- the human body reacts to low food intake by reducing its metabolic rate (i.e. your body goes into *starvation mode* to conserve energy); this defeats the point of the diet since it means that your body slows down your calorie consumption;
- constraining your food intake restricts your intake of **key nutrients** (e.g. vitamins and minerals), the absence of which can eventually make you ill;
- psychologically, dieting can reinforce a personal sense of **self-disgust** and dissatisfaction with your own body.

By contrast, losing fat by exercising increases your energy consumption, so that you can continue to eat normally, your body increases its metabolic rate (even when you are not running), you get plenty of key nutrients, and you feel good about yourself. For me it is a no-brainer: if you want to lose weight, take up running.

Do you really want to lose weight?

People who say they want to lose weight are usually using a shorthand for a number of different implicit and explicit goals. These might include:

- reducing visible **body fat**;
- improving **muscle tone**;
- increasing **muscle size**;

- reducing the appearance of **cellulite**;
- increasing **life expectancy** and reducing health risks such as heart disease and diabetes.

Very few of us, except perhaps professional athletes and horse jockeys, are really concerned about what we weigh. We are using body weight as a measure of our progress (or lack of it) towards underlying goals, which we are sometimes embarrassed to express openly.

But achieving lower levels of body fat and improving your appearance does not necessarily mean reducing your weight. Because muscle is made up of protein, which is heavier than fat, many people who begin to exercise find that they actually *increase* their weight, at least at first, as they build up their muscles, even though they are losing body fat. So despite increasing their weight, they are still achieving their goals of improving their appearance and reducing their body fat.

It is therefore important to be clear about what you are really trying to achieve. You may make good progress towards your goals without seeing any evidence in your weight or changes in your BMI. The danger is that you become too focused on losing weight and so make changes in your diet and lifestyle that make it harder, not easier, to achieve your real goals.

How to reduce your body fat

The principles for losing fat are simple. Your body uses fat to store energy that is surplus to its requirements. So if you take in (i.e. eat) more energy than you use up, your body will store the excess calories as fat. If you use up more energy than you take in, then you will burn stored fat to provide the extra energy.

From the point of view of reducing your body fat, it doesn't matter where the calories come from. A surplus calorie will be stored as body fat, whether it was originally from protein, carbohydrate or fat. So the composition of your food intake is much less important for losing fat than the total amount of calories you consume and the amount of energy you use.

In other words, **to reduce your body fat you must eat fewer calories *and/or* burn more energy**. This straightforward proposition has some important implications.

Eating and drinking fewer calories

Most **diets** are aimed at getting you to eat fewer calories. This usually means either restricting the total volume of food you eat, or eating foods that contain fewer calories per mouthful, so that you eat as much food but it contains less energy. (Some diets are intended to get you to burn more energy by increasing your metabolic rate – see below.)

It doesn't matter to your overall weight loss where the calories come from; but if you are going to restrict your calorie intake, it is generally a good idea to cut back on alcohol, harmful fats and refined sugars.

Alcohol is high in calories (about 90 kcal for a glass of wine or 170 kcal for a pint of beer). It is also diuretic (i.e. it makes you pee), contributing to dehydration. While alcohol is not unhealthy in moderation, it does not do you much good, and cutting back on calories from this source will make you less hungry than cutting back on your basic food intake.

The reasons for cutting back on **fats** are:

- fat has more than **twice as many calories per gram** than carbohydrates or protein; so if you cut back on calories by reducing fat, you don't have to reduce the amount of food you eat by so much as an equivalent reduction in calories achieved by cutting out protein or carbohydrate;
- some fats are **positively harmful** (see page 46–7) and so you should aim to reduce these in your diet;
- most of us **eat more fat than we should** in the first place; so cutting back on fat often brings us back towards a more desirable, balanced diet.

The reasons for cutting back on refined **sugars** are that they lead to large swings in blood sugar levels. In children, refined sugar is associated with hyperactivity.

This is not primarily a book about dieting. My view is that the best way to lose weight is to exercise more. But if you decide to cut back on calories, it seems that the most effective ways to do this are ones that don't leave you feeling perpetually hungry. This means that you need to eat foods that have high volume for each calorie. Hence low fat, low sugar, high fibre diets are likely to be the most sustainable ways to reduce calorie intake.

Burning more calories

Burning more calories is generally a more sustainable and positive way to lose body fat than trying to eat fewer calories. The main ways to burn more calories are to exercise, and to change what and when you eat.

Exercising burns more calories in three ways:

- first, you use energy during **the exercise itself**: for example, running or walking uses up about 100 calories per mile – and this is not greatly affected by how fast you go (clearly, you will burn more calories per hour if you run faster, but the number of calories per mile will stay pretty much the same); table 6.8 shows the calories burned for other common exercises;
- second, regular exercise increases your **metabolic rate** even while you are not exercising: essentially, if you exercise often your body adapts to a generally higher level of energy consumption;
- third, exercise increases the amount of **lean muscle tissue** in your body, and this in turn increases your metabolic rate.

Other ways to **increase your metabolic rate** (and hence energy consumption) are:

- altering **when you eat**: in general, a large breakfast seems to kick-start your metabolism so that you burn up more calories during the day;[29] in addition, there is evidence that eating little and often (e.g. 4–5 moderate-sized meals and snacks a day, rather than 2–3 larger meals) maintains a higher metabolic rate through the day;
- changing the **time you exercise**: exercising in the morning before you have breakfast may increase your metabolic rate during the day by more than exercise in the evening.

There may also be a marginal impact on your metabolism from changing **what you eat**. For example, your body seems to respond to carbohydrates by increasing your metabolism more than when you eat fats. However, the size of this effect is probably small enough to ignore.

How fast to reduce your body fat

If you do decide you want to reduce your body fat, you should not attempt to lose weight too rapidly. In particular, you should not aim to lose more than 0.5 kg a week; nor should you try to consume less than 85 per cent of your daily equilibrium calorie needs.

The best approach to estimating how fast you should be losing weight is:

- decide how much exercise you realistically intend to do;
- estimate your equilibrium daily calorie requirement (using the calculation on pages 49–50) at that level of exercise, given your current bodyweight;
- work out how many calories a day you need to eat to lose weight without consuming less than 85 per cent of your daily needs or losing more than 0.5 kg a week.

So, for example, if your equilibrium daily calorie requirement is 3000 kcal a day, you should not eat less than 2550 kcal (which is 85% of 3000). If you cut back to 2550 kcal a day, you will lose 3150 kcal a week – which is 350 g of fat (since fat weighs in at 9 calories per gram). This is the maximum realistic rate of weight loss for you.

Should you run more slowly to lose more fat?

You may have heard the claim that you should run more slowly to burn more fat. My local gym has signs declaring that there is a 'fat burning zone' in which anyone who is trying to lose weight is encouraged to stay.

This is an excellent example of Alexander Pope's dictum that 'a little learning is a dangerous thing.' As we shall see in the next chapter, it is true that the proportion of energy that comes directly from fat is higher at low rates of exercise intensity. But this doesn't mean that you are going to have less body fat if you exercise at lower intensities, for two reasons:

- first, it doesn't matter in the slightest for your overall level of body fat where the fuel comes from **while you are exercising**; your body will replenish and rebalance your energy stores when you are recovering. In the long run, a calorie surplus or deficit will always end up affecting your level of body fat, irrespective of which particular fuel was burnt during exercise;
- second, what matters is the **number** of calories that you burn. A higher **proportion** of the calories may come from fat if you run more slowly, but you are also burning fewer calories in total. If you only have so many hours in a day that you can devote to exercise, you will maximise the number of calories you expend by running as far and as fast as you can in those hours, not by going deliberately slowly.

As we shall see in chapters 9 and 10, there are good reasons for running slowly some of the time. But despite what you may have been told, it is not true that you will lose more weight this way.

Conclusion

A healthy, balanced diet is an essential component of any training programme. If you eat a wide variety of lightly processed or unprocessed foods, you won't go far wrong. You need also to ensure that you drink enough water.

Running is one of the healthiest, most sustainable ways to lose weight. Whereas diets are psychologically and often physically damaging, running is a positive and effective way to improve your appearance and health.

Running on the track improves your form

Eating and drinking before, during and after running

Chapter 6 explained the basic dietary requirements to support a healthy and active lifestyle. This chapter is about how you should eat and drink before, during and after running, and discusses the practicalities.

In general, you need to drink water and consume carbohydrates while running during runs that are longer than one hour or 10 km. For shorter runs, you are unlikely to need either, unless it is very hot in which case you may need water to prevent dehydration.

Water and dehydration

The dangers of dehydration and overhydration

As we saw in chapter 6, you need to consume about 1 litre of water for every 1000 kcal you consume. But in addition, you lose water through sweating when you exercise. A good rule of thumb is that you lose around half a litre for each hour that you exercise – and it can be substantially more than this if it is a hot day.

Some evidence shows that modest levels of dehydration lead to significant falls in athletic performance.[30] Your blood is about 82 per cent water. As you sweat more, your volume of blood is reduced, and your cardiovascular system works less efficiently at getting oxygen to your muscles. A loss of water equal to 2 per cent of your body weight (1½ litres for a 75 kg person) could reduce your aerobic capacity by up to 20 per cent.[31] Bigger sweat losses than this can lead to dangerous dehydration.

Contrary to the popular saying that 'women glow, men perspire and horses sweat', women also sweat while exercising, broadly the same amount as men (in proportion to bodyweight). So women should, like men, aim to replace the water they lose while exercising, either during the event (for longer events) or immediately afterwards.

In deciding how much to drink while exercising, however, you should take account of the fact that water is a by-product of burning fuel to produce energy. This means that your body is producing extra water internally when you are exercising, and you therefore don't need to drink to replace all the water you are losing through sweat.

You should be aware that it is possible to drink too much water, especially during endurance events. In one study of 17 runners who were hospitalised during the Comrades Marathon (an 89 km ultra-marathon in South Africa), nine had *hyponatraemia* (i.e. low blood sodium, associated with overhydration).[32] At least two marathon runners in the USA have died of hyponatraemia.

In a comprehensive discussion of this issue Tim Noakes concludes that distance runners should drink as they feel (and not force themselves to drink more), which generally means about 500 ml an hour.[33] However, other medical advice still recommends drinking rather more than this. For example, the American College of Sports Medicine recommends 600–1200 ml of sports drink an hour.[34] There is a danger that this may be too much for non-elite athletes who are running a marathon which takes them more than four or five hours. You will have to judge for yourself what works best for you, recognising that there are dangers from overhydration as well as from dehydration.

For running events of up to 10 km, it is unlikely that you will need to drink during the run unless the weather is exceptionally hot. But for longer events, including the marathon, your performance will suffer as a result of dehydration if you don't replace the water you are losing during the race.

Drinking before you run

One way to minimise dehydration is to ensure that you begin a run fully hydrated. In the days before a big race, it is a good idea to sip as much water as you can to keep your body topped up.

On the day of the run, drink up to two hours before the start. Most experienced runners stop then, to avoid the need to urinate while they are running.

You can begin drinking again immediately before the start. Marathon running writer Hal Higdon recommends drinking a can of Coke on the start line of a race.[35] Although this is a diuretic, it is unlikely to affect you during the race, and the caffeine jolt may help your performance.

Drinking while running

Drinking while running is a skill, and you need to practise it during your training to see what works best for you. Some tips are:

- drink little and often to avoid a bloated feeling while you are running;
- don't wait until you feel thirsty: by then you are already dehydrated. Get used to drinking from the beginning of the run;
- drink as you feel inclined, which should be about 500 ml every hour or a little more; if you are running a marathon and aim to complete it in four hours, this means about half of a paper cup of water every mile – but don't force yourself to drink too much;

Organised races over 5 km will usually provide water stations. Using these effectively is a skill that needs some practice:

- learn to take the cup from the helpers with your left hand; the water stations on the left side of the road tend to be less crowded than the water stations on the right;
- run on past the water station before you actually drink from the cup; you need to concentrate while running through the water station because runners will be weaving around and stopping suddenly in front of you, and there will be cups on the road; take time to walk for a few steps to enable you to drink comfortably and avoid choking;
- practise drinking from cups during your training; the best way to do this is to enter a local race and use it as a training run;
- be considerate to other runners coming after you: don't waste water, and dispose of your cup carefully.

On a hot day, you should regulate your temperature by splashing water over yourself as well as by drinking. You may want to pour a cup of water over your head (and especially down the back of your neck), and if you are wearing a cap, make it wet to keep you cool. During the closing stages of a race – for example, during the last half an hour – cooling yourself this way may be more effective than drinking.

Drinking after running

When you have finished running, you should aim to replenish the fluid you have lost. Because you don't absorb all the fluid you drink, it is recommended that you drink about half as much again as the volume of fluid you have lost.[36] After a long run, you should try to drink at least 500 ml immediately, and then the rest in slower time.

You should be able to urinate within six hours of completing a long run. If you cannot, it is possible that you have developed kidney failure. If you have not urinated within twelve hours of finishing a long run, contact a doctor. If you are developing kidney failure, the earlier you get medical help the better.[37]

Sports drinks

There is a growing range of drinks that can be used before, during and after exercise (including some other drinks marketed as 'sports drinks' with questionable nutritional credentials).

Reasons for drinking sports drinks

The main reasons for drinking sports drinks (as opposed to plain water) are:

- sports drinks are an effective way to replenish your body's **energy levels** by providing easily digestible carbohydrates;
- they may replace **essential minerals** (e.g. sodium, potassium, magnesium, chloride) that you lose when you sweat;
- dilute sugar solutions are **absorbed by the body more quickly than plain water**, so sports drinks can (depending on the concentration – see below) accelerate fluid replacement;
- drinks containing **sodium** increase the urge to drink and the palatability of the drink, thereby encouraging you to drink more.

Sports drinks are especially useful for endurance runners during long training runs and races (any run longer than an hour); and for shorter distance runners who want to replenish their energy stores after a tough workout.

Types of sports drinks

The concentration of a sports drink determines the effect it has on you, and the extent to which it speeds up water absorption. Broadly speaking, a drink with between 3 and 8 g of carbohydrate per 100 ml accelerates fluid absorption compared to plain water.

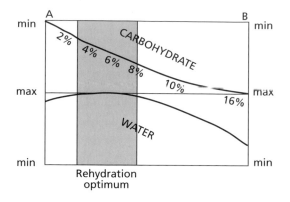

Relationship between concentration and absorption

Sports drinks are of three kinds:

- **isotonic** – the same concentration as normal bodily fluids and so easily absorbed; commercial isotonic drinks typically contain 4–8 g of carbohydrate per 100 ml. Isotonic drinks balance the need for rehydration and refuelling;
- **hypertonic** – more concentrated than normal bodily fluids; usually containing more than 8 g of carbohydrate per 100 ml; because of their concentration they are absorbed more slowly than isotonic drinks;
- **hypotonic** – less concentrated than normal bodily fluids; typically less than 4 g of carbohydrate per 100 ml. Absorbed faster than plain water, but containing less carbohydrate than isotonic drinks.

If the weather is hot, you should give more priority to fluid replacement, and choose a hypotonic or isotonic drink; in cooler conditions, you may find a hypertonic drink beneficial.

The optimum carbohydrates for sports drinks are glucose, maltose, glucose polymers (also known as maltodextrins) and soluble, branch-chained starches with high glycaemic indices (see chapter 6). Fructose, the sugar found in fruits, is not so well absorbed by the body during exercise, and can lead to an irritable stomach, but is fine in small quantities.

Glucose polymers are especially useful because they are molecules of carbohydrate in a form that does not add as much to the concentration of the drink as pure glucose. Because they are less sweet than simple sugars, they don't make a high-carbohydrate drink taste so sickly.

Some runners make their own drink from fruit juice, water and a little salt. This is fine if it works for you, though fructose (the sugar in fruit) is not easy to absorb.

Try to avoid drinks that contain sweeteners such as *aspartame* or *saccharine*, since these taste sweet but are not digested and so confuse the blood sugar regulation system.

What to look for in an ideal sports drink

1. **Palatability**
   The most scientifically formulated drink is of no value if it is so unpalatable that it cannot be drunk.

2. **Carbohydrate concentration of 5 to 10 per cent**
   Higher carbohydrate concentrations only become important near the end of prolonged, competitive exercise when the desire to drink falls, but the need for carbohydrate replacement is greatest.

3. **Carbohydrates from a variety of sources**
   A mixture of carbohydrate sources (glucose, fructose, maltodextrins) is necessary (i) to maximise palatability and (ii) to maintain a low-to-moderate osmolality [i.e. absorption rate] of the drink.

4. **Sodium concentration of 20 to 60 mmol.l-1**
   The higher sodium concentrations aid fluid balance when athletes are able to ingest fluid at high rates.

5. **All the rest is marketing**

   Tim Noakes, The Lore of Running, 2001

Energy for running

How your body stores energy

Your body stores energy as carbohydrates, fats and proteins, but the way energy is stored is not directly related to where the energy came from in the first place.

Carbohydrate is stored as glycogen in the muscles and liver. You can store up to about 400 g of glycogen in your muscles, and 100 g in your liver (though these can be increased with training). This means you can store about 2000 kcal as glycogen – enough energy to run or walk about 20 miles.

You store **fat** all over your body, particularly just beneath the skin and around your internal organs. The human body is, on average, about 15–25 per cent fat (i.e. about 10 kg for a 60 kg person) – though athletes tend to have a rather lower percentage body fat than the rest of the population.

Proteins are used as the body's building materials and are not generally used as the main source of energy, but your body can break down and use the energy from proteins in extreme circumstances.

How your body uses energy during exercise

Your body mainly uses carbohydrates and fats to provide energy during exercise. The precise mixture depends on the amount and type of exercise you do, how well trained you are, and on your inherited physiology.

The energy system used for all exercise lasting more than about 1½ minutes is called **aerobic** – which means that it uses oxygen. For short bursts of intense energy, the body uses **anaerobic** systems, which don't require oxygen but can only be sustained for short periods (e.g. sprints), and which (for all but very short bursts of energy) produce **lactic acid**.

The **aerobic energy system** primarily uses a combination of carbohydrates and fat (but can also use proteins). The proportion of carbohydrates and fats used depends on the intensity of the exercise. For low intensity exercise, your muscles mainly draw their energy from fat. But as your effort level goes up and your muscles have to generate energy more quickly, so you have to increase the proportion of energy that comes from carbohydrates. The proportion of energy provided from carbohydrates rises as exercise intensity increases from around 10 per cent to up to 90 per cent.

The carbohydrates used during exercise are stored as *glycogen* both in the muscles and around the liver. These stores are limited, and as they begin to run out the proportion of energy provided by fat rises (though you cannot metabolise fat unless there is some carbohydrate as well). Once your glycogen stores have run out, your body begins to break down muscle proteins to provide energy and to maintain blood sugar levels.

If you exercise very intensively, however, your aerobic metabolic system will not be sufficient to provide all the energy you need. At this point, your **anaerobic metabolism** is used to provide extra energy from glycogen. While this has the advantage of being very efficient at producing energy, and requiring no oxygen, it has the disadvantage of being very limited, and producing lactic acid as part of the process.

During training, you are aiming to increase your body's ability to turn fuel into energy by:

- teaching your body to become more efficient at converting fat into energy, so that you can exercise more intensively while still burning fat, thus protecting your (much more limited) stores of glycogen. This is one reason why the 'long, slow, distance run' is a key part of training for a marathon;
- increasing your body's ability to store glycogen, especially in the muscles, increasing your total carbohydrate stores.

Carbo-loading before a long run

For long races (longer than a half marathon), you need to ensure your glycogen stores are fully topped up at the start line. To do this, marathon runners indulge in what is known as 'carbo-loading' for the three days before the marathon. This means increasing the intake of carbohydrates – for example, pasta – in the run-up to the

---

Suggestions for carbo-loading

Breakfast
- breakfast cereal with raisins
- thick slices of toast with honey
- banana
- bagel with peanut butter
- pancakes

Lunch
- jacket potato with tuna, sweetcorn or cottage cheese
- rice salad with chicken or beans and vegetables
- banana sandwich
- fresh fruit

Dinner
- pasta with tomato sauce and lentils or cheese
- fresh vegetables
- fruit salad

Snacks
- toast with honey
- low-fat yoghurt or fromage frais
- low-fat rice pudding

---

race, while cutting back on running (and hence reducing glycogen consumption).

Years ago it was thought that carbo-loading should be preceded by a period of carbo-depleting, in which the body was starved of carbohydrates. This was thought to encourage the body to store carbohydrates during the loading phase. Subsequent studies showed that this is not effective, and athletes are no longer encouraged to deplete their glycogen before the carbo-loading phase. In addition, carbo-depletion can increase the risk of illness or injury, and makes many people irritable.

Carbo-loading should be accompanied by an increase in water consumption, partly because water is needed for the body to store glycogen, and partly because you should be increasing your water consumption anyway before a long race.

As we saw in chapter 6, the speed with which carbohydrates are absorbed into the bloodstream is measured by the *glycaemic index* (GI). In the six hours before you run, you should aim to eat a combination of foods that have a reasonably high glycaemic index, including, for example, bread, raisins and sugar, to increase your blood sugar and top up your body's glycogen stores. Examples of suitable meals on the day of the race are bread with honey, a baked potato with a low-fat filling, or pasta with tomato and lentil or tofu sauce, sprinkled with grated cheese.

Why you need to take in energy on long runs

If you run for less than an hour, you are unlikely to need to eat or drink while you are exercising. But for runs longer than an hour, your performance is likely to be improved if you top up your fuel as you go.

During the first hour of exercise, most of your energy comes from glycogen stored in your muscles. After about an hour, the muscles begin to draw their fuel from the blood sugar, which is in turn supplied by glycogen stored in your liver, as well as from their own stores. Your liver glycogen levels are also finite. So when your liver glycogen is depleted, your blood sugar level falls and you are unable to carry on exercising. This low blood sugar (called 'hypoglycaemia') induces a feeling of tiredness and light-headedness, and your legs begin to feel very heavy. Marathon runners know this as 'hitting the wall' or getting 'the bonks'. It is a quite distinct (and unpleasant) feeling, and it has the same effect on your running performance as a large bear climbing onto your back.

But if you can replenish your blood sugar while you are exercising, you will not deplete your liver glycogen stores so rapidly, with the result that you can carry on for longer before you hit the wall. That is why it is a good idea to take energy on runs of more than one hour.

How much energy you need while running

Research shows that the average person's muscles can take up about 30–60 g per hour of carbohydrate from the bloodstream.[38] So consuming more carbohydrate than this will not improve energy output or reduce fatigue. It takes about thirty minutes for the carbohydrate that you eat or drink to reach your bloodstream, so you need to start consuming carbohydrates *before* you begin to feel tired. The best strategy is to begin soon after you start your run.

For example, if you consume about 500 ml an hour of an isotonic sports drink containing 7 g of carbohydrate per 100 ml, then you will consume about 35 g of carbohydrate per hour, which will roughly maintain your blood sugar levels.

Gels

An alternative to using sports drinks to maintain your blood sugar levels is to use gels. These are sachets, sold in specialist running and fitness shops that contain a sugary syrup designed to be taken during long runs and races. Each sachet contains around 20 g of carbohydrate, so you can usefully take two or three each hour.

The main advantage of gel sachets is that they are easy to carry in a pocket, or tucked into your waistband. This means that you can take them on training runs as well as during a race, so that you can train using the same energy source as that which you will be using on the race day itself. (By contrast, you can't easily do this with a sports drink, since you would have to carry a lot of sports drink on your training runs.)

The gel sachets should be washed down with water (otherwise they are too concentrated and sickly), so most runners take them as they approach a water aid station. To get the right concentration, you need to wash down a full sachet with about 250 ml of water (more than a full paper cup). If this is too much water to drink in one go while you are running, then take less than a full sachet at each water station.

Well-known brands of gel include Squeezy™, Power Shots™, Cliff Shots™, Science in Sports™, and Gu™. They are all broadly the same (though some also contain caffeine) so try them all and see which you find most palatable. If you decide to use gels during a race, make sure that you use them on your long training runs as well, so that you can find out before the race if they are going to upset your stomach.

Energy after running

After you have finished running you should aim to restock your carbohydrate stores as quickly as possible. This will reduce the risk of illness. In addition, the more quickly you restock your glycogen stores, the more you develop your body's ability to store energy in this form.

In general, the principles for consuming energy after running are:

- aim to consume carbohydrates quickly – preferably **within half an hour**, and certainly within two hours; you may well not feel like eating straight away, but you should try to force yourself;
- consume **high glycaemic index carbohydrates**, which can be absorbed by the body quickly, such as a bagel with peanut butter, or a sports drink;
- drink **plenty of water** as well, since this is needed for storage of carbohydrates and to offset dehydration;
- try to accompany the carbohydrates with some **protein and fats**, since this aids absorption of the carbohydrates. A baked potato with beans or tuna is ideal.

In other words, the best foods to eat immediately after a long run are roughly the same as you should eat before it: plenty of high glycaemic carbs with a little protein, washed down with lots of water.

Conclusion

For any runs of 10 km or more, and when the weather is hot, you need to drink while running to avoid dehydration. And for any run over half a marathon, or over two hours, you should also aim to take in some energy while you are running. This will make the run more pleasurable, aid your recovery and (if you are racing) improve your performance.

This chapter may have given you the impression that there is a lot to remember, and a lot of numerical calculations. Don't be put off: just experiment and find out what works best for you.

⑧ Injuries

Whenever runners are gathered together, they talk about injuries: injuries they have had, injuries they have got now and injuries that explain the absence of mutual friends.

So if runners are always injured, running must be bad for you, right? Wrong. Running is good for you. However, runners often push themselves near to their limits, which means that, although they are in generally better shape than couch potatoes, they get more injuries than they would if they spent their day watching TV. Because runners are stubborn, and sometimes a little obsessed, they often don't do what they should to avoid injuries, and they don't treat them properly when they occur.

Overuse injuries

Runners often suffer from injuries that can be loosely grouped together as 'overuse' injuries – that is, they are not caused by an external force or accident, but appear to be the result of many miles and hours of running. As we shall see in this chapter, many of these injuries are caused by (often minor) biomechanical imbalances and defects that, when combined with running, lead to stresses on joints, muscles and other tissues. The cure for these injuries is very rarely found by addressing the symptoms: instead it is necessary to identify the underlying problem.

The trouble is not that we run too much; just the opposite. Because so many of us have sedentary lifestyles, including long hours sitting in chairs, we develop weaknesses and imbalances that then cause problems when we run. So the underlying cause of overuse injuries is generally not running (though it is running that triggers the symptoms), but the deterioration in the strength and flexibility in our bodies that prevents us from running efficiently and without pain. Fortunately, many of these problems are easy to fix, if you get the right advice and tackle the underlying causes rather than the symptoms. Sadly, all too few doctors know how to do this.

There are seven main overuse injuries which affect runners.

Runner's knee

Runner's knee is the usual description for pain just below the kneecap. The pain occurs at first during running, and gradually gets worse. Walking up or down stairs, and squatting, cause pain. Sitting with the knee bent for a long time – such as in the cinema – also causes discomfort. These symptoms are the result of bruising near the bottom of the kneecap, which may be caused by incorrect tracking of the kneecap as you run.

Runner's knee is usually caused by overpronation, often combined with inappropriate running shoes or excessive increases in training load. Because of the different alignment of the pelvis and legs, runner's knee is more common in women than men.

Runner's knee is often misdiagnosed by non-running doctors as *chondromalacia patella*, which is a deterioration of the cartilage in the knee joint, or as damage to the back of the knee-cap. If your doctor or physio says that you have damaged cartilage, you should get a second opinion from an experienced sports doctor before proceeding with the recommended treatment.

Once correctly diagnosed, runner's knee can be corrected by fixing the biomechanical problems that caused it. Studies have shown that up to 80 per cent of runners with this condition can be cured by the use of orthotics (see pages 80–1).[39]

Iliotibial band (ITB) friction syndrome

This manifests itself as severe pain on the outside of the knee joint, which becomes worse as you run. The pain often stops as soon as you stop running. The iliotibial band is a band of tissue that runs from the hip, down the outside of the thigh, past the knee, and connects to the lower leg. It helps to keep the knee joint stable.

ITB friction syndrome occurs when the band becomes irritated as it rubs over a bony prominence near the knee (technically the lateral epicondyle of the femur) which it passes over as you bend your leg at the knee. ITB friction syndrome is often caused by excessive ankle pronation, but there are other possible causes, including tightness of the tensor fasciae latae muscle, or unequal leg length which tilts the pelvis. It can be exacerbated by increasing training too rapidly, or running downhill or on heavily cambered roads.

The symptoms are alleviated by stretching the ITB band (see page 78), ice and deep friction massage. Treatment may require a reduction in training mileage and intensity, or complete rest while the underlying causes are addressed.

Achilles tendonitis

The Achilles tendon runs down the back of your heel, connecting the calf muscles to the heel. Achilles tendonitis begins as an inflammation of this tendon, but if left untreated it can develop into a rupture of the tendon. In its early stages, the symptoms are stiffness behind the ankle when you get out of bed in the morning. The symptoms often disappear while you are running.

Achilles tendonitis is typically caused by excessively tight calf muscles, overpronation, wearing high heels, worn-out shoes and overtraining. The symptoms can be relieved with ice after each run; but reduction in training or complete rest may be needed while the causes are addressed. It is generally advisable to avoid hills and speed work while you have Achilles tendonitis.

Shin splints

All too often, any pain in the lower leg is lazily described as 'shin splints'. The term is correctly used to describe *medial tibial stress syndrome*, which is an irritation of the muscles and tendons at the point where they attach to the shin bone (tibia).

Shin splints cause pain along the inner border of the shin, about 5–10 cm above the ankle. At first, the pain may be felt at the beginning of a run; sometimes it recedes as the workout continues, and then recurs afterwards; in other cases it is felt only at the end of the run. In the early stages the pain usually disappears after several minutes' rest. As the injury gets worse, the pain becomes more severe, sharper, and more persistent, until eventually it becomes difficult to walk normally.

This injury is quite common in new runners (often within their first three months of running) who have increased their training load too rapidly, or who are using inappropriate running shoes. It can also be caused by uncorrected ankle pronation.

Treatment at first includes regular ice, together with reduced mileage, running only on soft surfaces, or rest. Addressing the causes is likely to include ensuring that shoes have adequate cushioning and stability, and building up training mileage slowly.

Stress fractures

Stress fractures are hairline fractures of bones in the lower leg, usually the tibia, fibula or a bone in the foot (e.g. a metatarsal), though they can also occur in the thigh bone and pelvis. Stress fractures generally become painful very rapidly, and they can be identified by exquisite, highly localised pain under gentle pressure.

Stress fractures are usually caused by excessive increases in training or low bone density, possibly related to poor diet. They are more common in females than in males, and women with irregular menstrual cycles are especially at risk (see chapter 4).

This injury heals itself with two to three months of complete rest.

Muscle tears

These are extremely common injuries among runners. Muscle tears can occur suddenly – most commonly in explosive sports such as sprinting or football – or accumulate slowly over time. The hamstrings, groin and calf muscles are most at risk from muscle tears.

Sudden muscle tears are easy to diagnose: the runner suddenly feels severe pain in the affected muscle, which goes into spasm and swells up. The muscle cannot be used at all. Sudden muscle tears are caused by muscular imbalances, and exercising while insufficiently warmed up. The symptoms should be treated immediately with ice and elevation, and the application of a firm compression bandage immediately after icing. With intensive treatment an athlete can return to running in as little as a fortnight; though recovery generally takes a bit longer for non-elite athletes.

With gradual muscle tears, or 'muscle knots', by contrast, the pain comes on gradually. At first, symptoms are noticeable after exercise, and they are mild enough to continue training. Over time the pain becomes worse and eventually prevents running altogether. To identify a muscle tear for certain, a doctor or physio should press the affected muscle with two fingers: he or she will feel a small knot in the muscle, which, when pressed, causes excruciating pain to the runner.

Gradual muscle tears will not go away without the correct treatment, which is cross-friction massage by a physiotherapist. (Good luck: this hurts.) Five to ten sessions, lasting about ten minutes, will generally be enough.

Gradual muscle tears tend to recur in the same places. Runners need to be especially careful to stretch those muscles, especially before speed workouts and when it is cold. At the first sign of the symptoms returning, you should get more massage.

Plantar fasciitis

This injury manifests itself as pain directly in front of the heel, which can radiate down the arch or up the back of the heel. The pain is often worse when you first get out of bed. It generally hurts at the start of a run, but goes away when you are warmed up.

Plantar fasciitis is the result of stress and inflammation of the fibrous tissue in the bottom of the foot, called the *plantar fasciia*. It is usually caused by overpronation, or poor flexibility in the calves or hamstrings. It is also more common in people who are overweight.

Initially, treatment is aimed at stretching the tight plantar fascia and calf muscles, cushioning the heel, and decreasing inflammation with ice or anti-inflammatory drugs.

Avoiding injury

Overuse running injuries are not caused by bad luck; and runners should not be fatalistic about them. Most are caused by an identifiable and avoidable biomechanical problem, often excessive ankle pronation. You cannot completely eliminate the risk of injury – but there are some key steps you can take to reduce the risks.

Five steps for avoiding injury

First, **start running slowly**. People who are new to running and try to do too much too soon will usually become injured, often in their third month of running (see chapter 2 for more information about starting out).

Second, get **the right running shoes**. By far the biggest cause of overuse injuries is overpronation, which can usually be corrected by choosing appropriate running shoes. Unfortunately, many sports shops don't know how to sell you the right shoes. (See chapter 3 for more information about buying shoes.)

Third, get a **check-up by a sports physiotherapist and podiatrist**. This may sound excessive for a hobby runner, but it could well save you from considerable pain, frustration and expensive treatments later. A good sports clinic will make a videotape of you running on a treadmill, and use this to assess your running pattern (sometimes called *gait analysis*). They can then give you exercises and stretches that will partially correct your biomechanical imperfections, and so greatly reduce the risk of injury.

Fourth, **stretch**. Maintaining flexibility will reduce your risk of injury. (Stretching is so important that it is discussed more fully further on in this chapter.)

Fifth, **never just 'run through' pain**. As you become a more experienced runner you will learn to distinguish the normal aches and pains that are associated with hard training and effort, and pain that is your body's way of telling you that there is something wrong. When you experience discomfort, don't just keep running and hope that it will go away – the chances are that it will become worse. Nor should you simply stop running – whatever caused the problem will do so again when you return to running. See a specialist who can help to identify the cause, so that you can tackle it (often a straightforward matter of different shoes, simple exercise and stretches, or orthotics in your shoes) before it creates a serious problem.

'Soon after I started running, just as I was really starting to enjoy it, I had to stop for six months because of injury. First I got tendonitis in my groin because I pushed myself too hard every time I went running, instead of interspersing easy runs between hard sessions. Then I got an inflamed Achilles tendon because I increased my mileage too rapidly. Looking back, I wish I had been more patient and built up a firm base of fitness, and invested more in what may seem like side issues, such as flexibility and core stability before trying to build up my mileage. And because I'm relatively new to running, I've realised I should concentrate on shorter distances at first. The main lesson for me is that you have to listen to your body – if it hurts all the time you are doing something wrong. One week's missed training is better than 6 months moping about not being able to run at all.'

Matt Siddle, 24

Core stability

The biomechanical weaknesses that cause overuse injuries occur primarily because our lifestyles are not consistent with the range of activities for which the human body evolved. For example, because the average city dweller spends large parts of every day sitting down, his or her thigh muscles (*quadriceps*) become elongated and hamstrings too short. Because of our lack of physical activity, muscles are underused and become too weak, or are sometimes not fired (*recruited*) at all.

You may be thinking to yourself that none of this applies to you, because you are fit, you run and you go regularly to the gym. You are very likely in a better position than the average sedentary person. But we are increasingly coming to understand that the dynamic exercises we do while running or working out address only part of the problem.

Some physiotherapists suggest that we need to pay more attention to our **core stability** – that is, the ability of key muscles around the abdomen, pelvis and back to hold the torso steady. The muscles that do this are not the large surface muscles that are used in dynamic exercises such as sit-ups or leg curls. They are deeper muscles, designed to work statically (that is, they prevent rather than generate movement). In people who get injured, it appears that these muscles fire late, or not at all, and are too weak to perform their stabilising function. Annoyingly, the exercises most of us do in the gym to strengthen our trunk (e.g. sit-ups or trunk curls) target the wrong muscles because they are dynamic. Indeed, they may even do the opposite, because the dynamic muscles dominate, allowing the static muscles to become lazy and atrophy.

It is clear that having good biomechanics depends on the proper functioning of these key muscles around our lower trunk, and on all our muscles being properly recruited, the right length and sufficiently strong and flexible.

Specialists often ascribe running injuries to **overpronation**. The implication is sometimes that, with the right pair of shoes or inserts, the problem will go away; or that the injured runner should simply give up because they are not cut out for running. But overpronation is itself a symptom of some other problem, which could be anywhere from your abdomen down to your big toe. Once diagnosed, it is often easy to fix (and better shoes or inserts may well be part of the solution). But if you have an injury and your therapist seems to be tackling only the symptoms, try to find one who looks for the underlying cause and helps you to fix that, or you will find yourself going back time and time again.

Core stability is a deceptively simple but important idea. It tells us that we should look for the causes of injuries, not in our running, which is consistent with the evolution of the human body over millions of years, but in the weaknesses and imbalances in our bodies caused by the lifestyles we live today for which our bodies are not well adapted.

Treating minor injuries

It is difficult to generalise about what you should do if you get an injury – so much depends on the nature of the injury and the probable cause.

For minor niggles that you can treat yourself, remember the golden rule: **RICE – Rest, Ice, Compression and Elevation**.

For anything that lasts more than a day or two, or that causes severe discomfort, pins and needles, paralysis, sharp localised pain, or discoloration, seek medical help as quickly as possible.

Rest

A general guideline is that if you have aches and niggles that don't hamper your running performance, you can probably go on running. But if you have discomfort that you would describe as pain, or if your running is affected, then you probably need to ease back or stop running.

Ice

Ice any inflammation early and often. It increases blood flow to the injured area, reducing swelling and dramatically speeding healing. The first time you try it, you will be surprised at how effective this is at accelerating the healing of minor knocks.

(As I was writing this chapter, I hit my leg against a rubbish bin while out running, and caused a nasty bruise on my lower leg that made it difficult to walk. With rapid and repeated icing, the bruise had gone by the next day.)

To ice an injury, use a bag of ice cubes or a bag of frozen peas, wrapped in a damp tea towel to avoid ice-burn, for fifteen minutes. (You should not ice for longer than this, or your body will begin to cut off the blood supply to the iced area, which is the opposite of what you want. You also risk getting frostbite.) You should ice an injury as quickly as you can after the injury, and repeat up to once an hour.

Compression

For inflamed muscles and joints you can use a pressure bandage, which you can buy at your local chemist. This will help to reduce the swelling and speed recovery.

Elevation

Finally, you should try to raise the injured part of your body above your heart – for example, by stretching your leg out on the armrest of a couch. At night, try putting telephone directories under the legs at the foot end of the bed, so as to create a slight slope down towards your head.

Other treatments

Other treatments for minor injuries include:

- **anti-inflammatory drugs** such as aspirin, ibuprofen. In the US these are often called non-steroid anti-inflammatory drugs (NSAIDs). They can be useful to reduce inflammation in the short run, which can help to accelerate recovery. They may also help blood flow to repair microscopic muscle damage caused by long runs. But you should not get into the habit of taking anti-inflammatory drugs regularly, since this may simply mask a serious injury. Prolonged use of anti-inflammatory drugs can also contribute to damage to the kidneys, and in extreme cases kidney failure;
- **ultrasound** – this is a high-frequency wave that is applied by a trained professional (e.g. a doctor or physiotherapist). It can help to stimulate blood flow, and break up bruising and clots;
- **massage** by a sports masseur or physiotherapist can help to improve blood flow and to realign muscle fibres. This is discussed in more detail below.

Stretching

The benefits of stretching

The jury is still out on the benefits of stretching. The current wisdom is that static stretching *before* you train is unlikely to be beneficial, and may even be harmful; but that stretching *after* you run may improve muscle recovery and reduce muscle soreness. You should, however, warm up before running hard (see page 116).

In addition, as many runners who stretch will attest, maintaining flexibility makes you *feel* better, improves running performance and reduces the long-run risk of injury. Stretching can also contribute to a programme of developing core stability, by correcting imbalances in muscle length that lead to poor biomechanics. So in general, runners should stretch more, though they don't need to combine stretching in the same workout as running.

A particular problem for runners, because of the repetitive nature of the sport, is hamstrings and calf muscles that are too short and need stretching. These problems are reinforced by the fact that many of us spend much of the day sitting down, which leaves these muscles in a short position. This can often result in injury, including hamstring strains and Achilles tendonitis (see pages 68–71).

How to stretch

Most people prefer to stretch warm muscles, and do some light jogging or cycling to warm up before they stretch. However, there is no evidence that warm muscles can be stretched more easily than cold muscles, nor that warming up before stretching reduces the risk of injury.

The days of bouncing up and down to touch your toes are, mercifully, over. Rapid movements trigger a 'stretch reflex' in the muscle being stretched, which causes it to contract. Just as you are trying to lengthen the muscle, it is trying to contract, and you will put undue stress on the muscle. **So you are at considerable risk of injury if you try to stretch by bouncing up and down**.

Instead, you should gradually stretch out the muscle, and hold the stretch while breathing deeply. After 20 seconds or so, the muscle tension falls, and you should be able to stretch the muscle a little more. Remember to breathe deeply, and push the stretch a little further as you breathe out. Hold the stretch for about 60 seconds in total for each muscle.

Don't expect immediate results from stretching. The benefits take time to build up. But once you have increased your flexibility, it can be maintained with much reduced levels of stretching.

Key stretches for runners

The most important stretches for runners are the hamstrings, calves, quadriceps, back, hip flexors, groin, and iliotibial band.

Hamstrings

The hamstring runs from the buttocks down to just below the knee. The hamstring is the muscle that lifts the lower leg and bends the knee after the quads have lifted your knees.

- Lie on your back, bending both legs and keeping the small of the back on the ground. Look upwards. Lift your right knee up so that the thigh is at right angles to the floor, and grasp the back of the right thigh with both hands, near the knee joint. Then slowly straighten your right leg at the knee until you feel the stretch.
- Hold for 30 seconds and then change legs.

Hamstrings

Calf: Gastroc

The gastrocnemius muscle is the larger calf muscle.

Gastroc stretch

- Stand in front of a wall, with your feet parallel to each other, and the toes pointing straight forwards.
- Take one step forwards with your right leg (keeping the feet parallel).
- Lean forwards against the wall, on both palms. Your left foot is now behind you; keep the heel on the ground and try to keep a good arch in your right foot.
- Keep your back straight, and imagine a straight line from your neck, down your back, through your buttocks and leg to your ankle. Don't rotate the top of your pelvis forwards.
- Lean forward until you feel the stretch in the calf of your left leg. Hold for 30 seconds, and then switch to the soleus stretch (below).

Calf: Soleus

The soleus is the other major muscle in the calf.

- From the gastroc stretch, keep your back straight and your feet parallel and pointing forwards. Remember to keep the arch of the back foot up. Move your hands from the wall and put them on your hips. Then bend your legs as if you were going to sit down on an imaginary chair. Keep both heels flat on the ground. You may need to move the front foot back towards you a bit to keep your balance.
- You should feel the stretch in your lower calf. Hold the stretch for 30 seconds, then go back to gastroc stretch with the other leg.

Soleus stretch

Quads

The quadriceps are the muscles on the front of the thigh. They are used to straighten the leg.

- Stand straight with your feet and knees together. You may want to hold on to a partner or a wall for balance. Bend your left leg at the knee. Reach back with the left hand and hold the ankle (not the toes).
- Your knees should stay together, and your left thigh should be pointing straight down. Keep your back straight and tuck your bottom in. For an extra stretch in your quads, clench your buttocks together.
- Feel the stretch in your left quads and hold for 30 seconds. Then change legs.

Quads

Lower back

This stretches your lower back.

- Lie on your back. Bring both knees to the chest. Grasp both knees with both hands, pull them down to the chest.
- Feel the stretch in your lower back. Hold it for 30 seconds.

Back

Hip flexors

You have a hip flexor on each leg, connecting the lower spine and the hip bone to the top of the thigh. Their main action is to lift the leg forwards.

Hip flexors

- Take a long step forwards with your right leg, and let your left leg drop so that the knee is on, or just off, the floor.
- Your right knee should bend in a line with the second toe of your right foot, but the right foot should be ahead of the left knee.
- Keep your upper body straight and look straight ahead. Arch your shoulders back slightly. You may want to put your hands behind your back.
- You should feel the stretch on your left hip. Hold the stretch for 30 seconds, then change legs and repeat.

Groin

This stretch reaches the groin on both sides.

- Sitting, bend both legs and put the soles of your feet together. Hold your feet with both hands. Pull your lower back forwards to keep your back straight. With your elbows push out against the insides of your knees.
- You should feel the stretch in your inner thighs. Hold it for 30 seconds.

Groin

Iliotibial band

The iliotibial band runs from the hip, down the side of the leg, past the knee to the lower leg.

Iliotibial band

- Cross your feet by putting the left foot in front of the right foot. Find your balance and keep your back straight. Bend the left leg slightly, and keep the right leg straight.
- Push the right hip to your right, away from the centre of your body. Keep your hands by your sides. You should feel the stretch on the outside of your right leg.
- Hold the stretch for 30 seconds, then change legs and repeat.

Massage

Regular massage reduces injury and improves performance. It does this by stimulating blood flow to muscles that are recovering, helping to expel waste and toxins and bringing fresh nutrients needed to rebuild body tissue. It also has psychological benefits, by increasing the runner's sense of well-being and relaxation. If you can afford regular massages, they will help your running performance.

Massage can also be used to treat minor muscular injuries, such as muscle tears. A good sports masseur will find the site of the injury and apply **cross-friction massage** – an extremely painful but very effective treatment. (This is one of the very few cases in which the old phrase *if it ain't hurtin', it ain't workin'* is actually true.)

Physiotherapy, podiatry and orthotics

There is a saying among old cynics that 'doctors are people you pay to distract you while nature heals your problem'. Many runners think that their physiotherapist is someone they pay a lot for the privilege of being watched while they heal.

If you run regularly you will eventually have some kind of injury or niggle that might warrant the attention of a physiotherapist or podiatrist. What's the difference? **Physiotherapists** are dedicated to restoring and maintaining the physical function of the body. **Podiatrists** diagnose and treat disorders, diseases and injuries of the foot and lower leg.

If you have a running injury, it really is worth seeing a good sports physio and podiatrist. This will reduce the time it takes to recover, through advice and treatment (such as massage and ultrasound). It is true that, if you rest, the symptoms of most injuries will disappear over time of their own accord. But the main point in seeing a physio is to get a diagnosis of the underlying problem that caused the injury in the first place.

'The best way to find a good physio is to ask for a recommendation from a fellow runner. In the course of 18 months, I suffered four episodes, of about 3–4 weeks each, during which I couldn't run because of pain in my Achilles tendon. On the first three occasions, I tried three different physios, each of whom treated the symptoms, thus enabling me to run again – only for the problem swiftly to recur. And each time, the pain got worse. The fourth time it happened, I was fortunate enough to have a friend who recommended a new physio. This physio refused to treat the symptoms – at least until he had identified and addressed the underlying problem. Since he treated me, I haven't had any further problems with my ankle.'

Rebecca Stubbs, 30, Great Britain age-group triathlete

How to find a physiotherapist

You may be able to persuade your doctor to refer you to a physiotherapist: in this case your physio treatment will be paid for by the National Health Service. However, an NHS physio is unlikely to be a specialist in sports injuries, and there may well be a long waiting list.

If you have private health insurance, you will need to get a referral by your doctor, and you will need to check that the physio you want to see has been approved by your health insurer. Alternatively, you can pay for your own physio appointments, which costs £30–50 for a half-hour appointment.

Your local running club or specialist running shop should be able to point you in the direction of a good physiotherapist. You should look for a physio who:

- runs, or is at least physically active; there is little worse than a physio who does not understand your need to get back to running as soon as possible;
- looks for the underlying causes of the injury rather than just treating the symptoms, and looks at the alignment of your entire body, not just at the site of the symptoms;
- works in tandem with a podiatrist, so that you can get an expert opinion on the mechanics of your foot, and, if necessary, inserts for your shoes.

Podiatrists

Podiatrists specialise in the treatment of feet and lower limbs. They can help you to identify, cure and (importantly) prevent problems with your lower leg that may result in injuries. A particularly common problem is overpronation of the ankle, which, as we have seen above, can cause a variety of injuries. Overpronation can often be solved by selecting an appropriate model of running shoe; or by using orthotic inserts in your running shoes. Other treatments that a podiatrist might provide include manipulating or massaging the feet or legs, or recommending particular muscle strengthening exercises or stretches.

A good podiatrist will work with a physiotherapist to ensure that a proper diagnosis is made, not only of any shortcomings in your feet, ankles and lower legs, but more generally, so that you identify and tackle contributory factors elsewhere.

Orthotic shoe inserts

Although running shoes can help to limit biomechanical deficiencies, they cannot always do so if the problem is acute, or much more pronounced on one side than the other. One increasingly common solution is the use of orthotic shoe inserts, which are designed to fit inside your shoe and help to control the way the foot moves when it hits the ground. (These are properly called *orthoses* or *orthotic shoe inserts* but they are generally known as *orthotics*.)

Orthotics can be bought off the shelf, designed for runners with common symptoms. These are widely available in running shops and chemists, and are quite cheap. Alternatively, orthotics can be purpose-made for the individual runner. These can be quite expensive – about £100–200 for a pair – though they last a long time and can be transferred from one pair of shoes to another. To get purpose-made orthotics you need to go to a podiatrist, who will take plaster casts of your feet.

The design of orthotics varies; the most common are *arch supports* that stabilise the foot and ankle; but there are other inserts for specific conditions, such as *heel cups* (which go under the heel to relieve plantar fasciitis) and *metatarsal cushions* (which go just behind the toes to relieve pain in the forefoot).

Infections

Impact of running on immunity

It appears that moderate exercise increases resistance to disease and infections; but that heavy training and racing weakens the immune system. Mild exercise raises the body temperature and stimulates production of white blood cells and so helps the body to fight infection.[40] In general, the higher level of fitness in runners reduces their overall rates of infection and disease.

However, there is considerable evidence that susceptibility to infection is increased by running marathons. For example, 13 per cent of the runners who completed the Los Angeles Marathon in 1987 became ill during the week after the race, compared to just 2 per cent of the control group of runners who didn't participate in the event.[41] It is not clear why runners are especially prone to respiratory infections such as sore throats and bronchial infections. It may be to do with the trauma to the throat linings of hard breathing while running. But there also appears to be a lowering of the effectiveness of the immune system generally in runners who are training hard, which contributes to this phenomenon.

My own experience is that respiratory infections are the main constraint on my ability to train hard enough to improve my performance. So for some runners, finding ways to reduce the likelihood of infections is especially important for improving their running, as well as general quality of life.

Avoiding infection

The main approaches to reducing infection are:

- ensure you have a **good diet** – you need to eat a wide selection of fresh fruit and vegetables, and get enough essential minerals (especially zinc);
- avoid **swings in your blood sugar level**, which appear to cause reduced immunity; in general you should eat low glycaemic carbohydrates (except when you want a sugar boost, such as immediately before or after a long run). And if you eat a snack that is high in carbohydrates (e.g. fruit) make sure you have some protein with it (e.g. a handful of nuts);
- take a **vitamin C supplement**: take about 2000–4000 mg a day when you are training heavily; and increase this to 1000 mg an hour (really) if you feel as if you are becoming ill; although there is an upper limit beyond which increases in Vitamin C don't help, it does not appear to be harmful, even in very large doses. It can, however, lead to diarrhoea, and taking too much Vitamin C can burn a nasty hole in your pocket;
- take a **zinc supplement**; however, unlike Vitamin C, it is dangerous to take excessive doses of zinc, so restrict yourself to 100 mg a day;
- some runners find that **Echinacea extracts**, available in chemists and health food shops, improve their immune system;

- avoid **rapid increases in your training load**; build up slowly, increasing by not more than 10 per cent or two miles a week (whichever is the greater);
- don't do **two hard training sessions** on consecutive days;
- avoid **crowded buses, trains and tubes** if possible, for example by running, cycling or walking to work; and wash your hands regularly to avoid infection;
- make sure you **get enough sleep**.

Infection while tapering

As we shall see in chapter 11, long distance runners generally reduce their training mileage immediately before a big race. This is called 'tapering'.

Many runners are especially susceptible to infections when they are tapering. This phenomenon has not been researched, but paradoxically it appears to be a response to the reduced stress the body is under as you cut back your training load. This is analogous to the tendency many people have to fall ill on the first few days of a holiday. It may also be that you begin tapering just after the peak of your training load, so any infection is a delayed response to earlier stresses your body was under. The effect is especially disruptive, because the runner becomes ill just at the time at which he or she wants to conserve energy and health.

To avoid illness in the tapering phase, you should follow the guidelines above for avoiding infection. But you should also continue to train during the tapering phase, and maintain **high levels of effort**, albeit over smaller distances, to prevent the body from 'shutting down'.

Running with an infection

Runners often want to know whether it is safe to continue running if they have a sore throat, cold or cough.

In general, it is safe to continue running if you feel like it, provided that your body temperature is normal and that all the symptoms are from the neck upwards. You should not run if your temperature or resting heart rate are elevated, you have aching muscles or sore joints, or diarrhoea, or a chest infection. If your symptoms are nothing more than a sore throat or a runny nose, you can go out for an easy run. If your head starts to pound or if you don't feel well, turn round and go home.

My experience is that it is better to rest if you don't feel well. You are likely to lose less running overall if you let your body recover and get back to full strength quickly than if you try to train through an infection, and prolong the time it takes you to recover. If you do run with a cold, take it easy. Don't do a hard track session, or a long run. It is essential to drink more fluids if you have any kind of infection, as these help your body to recover.

Exercising while you are infected with a virus can be especially dangerous, since it can lead to an infection of the heart called *myocarditis*. You should not exercise at all if you have symptoms of a viral infection (such as fever, aching muscles or sore joints), and you should avoid vigorous exercise for a fortnight after your body temperature returns to normal. You should not exercise at all if your resting heart rate remains elevated. Myocarditis can cause severe damage to your heart and is sometimes fatal. If you might have a viral infection, don't even think about running.

Overtraining

We all want to achieve more. Runners, in particular, appear to be driven to test themselves, and push themselves to the limit of what they can achieve. This gives rise to the most common illness of athletes: overtraining. This syndrome gives rise to a number of different symptoms, all of which are strong indicators of overtraining.

It is essential for runners to recognise the symptoms of overtraining. If a runner at risk of overtraining backs off immediately, a rest of 24–48 hours will usually be sufficient. But if you ignore the early signs, and continue to overtrain, you will need 6–12 weeks off running to recover properly.

The best way to track possible overtraining is to keep a comprehensive training log that includes your weight, the number of hours you sleep, and your pulse rate both when you wake up and when you get out of bed. Monitor these indicators carefully, especially when your training load is at its highest.

One especially good early warning indicator of overtraining is the gap between your heart rate when you first wake up, and your heart rate after you have got out of bed. Your heartbeat generally increases by about 5 beats a minute when you get up. The gap is different from person to person, but is generally fairly constant from one day to the next. However, it can increase noticeably if you are in the early stages of overtraining. If you are susceptible to overtraining, then monitor this difference every day, and if the gap is 5 bpm or more above average, don't train that day.

According to Tim Noakes:

'the overtraining syndrome is caused by a very major disruption to the body's ability to respond to normal stresses such as infection and running. It is possible that this quite gross abnormality represents a protective response of a totally exhausted body. Rather than suffer additional damage that would result if the body were allowed to continue training in this depleted state, the body responds by making training impossible. We must learn to respect the messages that our bodies give us when they are trying to tell us that they have done too much.' [42]

Symptoms of overtraining

- increased resting heart rate;
- increase in difference between heart rate before and after getting out of bed;
- susceptibility to infections, allergies, headaches; swollen glands;
- sharp reduction in training performances; sluggishness;
- lethargy; loss of enthusiasm, energy or drive;
- irritability, loss of concentration;
- insomnia;
- loss of appetite;
- lack of sexual energy and loss of libido;
- rapid weight loss;
- diarrhoea and runners' trots.

Conclusion

This chapter has been all about learning to listen to our bodies.

We runners don't do ourselves very many favours. Although we know running does us good, it also mercilessly exposes imbalances or weaknesses in our bodies. As Noakes says, 'running injuries are not an Act of God'.[43] They are avoidable, if we take care of ourselves and take simple steps to keep our bodies in good shape and in proper balance. As we get injured, we need to look beyond the symptoms, and understand the underlying causes. Whatever your friends and your doctor might tell you, the problem is not that you are doing 'too much running'. If you can establish the true underlying causes of your injury now, you will save weeks, months or even years of pain and frustration in the future.

Understanding our bodies better is also the key to preventing overtraining. The obstinacy and stubborn determination of runners is so often a great strength of character. Through our training, we seek to develop in ourselves the mental toughness that we need to get out of bed for a training run on a dark winter morning, or to keep running through the last six miles of a marathon. But this discipline can also lead us to ignore the messages that our bodies give us when we are at our physical limits. An integral part of maturing as a runner is learning to listen to the complex messages that our bodies send us, and being able to recognise when we are trying to do too much.

Training cookbook: the ingredients

There are rites of passage in every runner's life: the first time you put on a pair of training shoes; your first injury; joining a running club; entering your first race; and the day you run your first marathon.

One of the milestones that you, like every runner, will pass is when you realise that, to improve your performance and enjoyment of running, you need to begin to train at different paces. So instead of just stepping out of your front door every day for your run – same distance, same speed – you begin to introduce variation into your timetable: long, slow runs, or shorter, sharper sessions designed to increase your strength or speed. As well as increasing the variety and pleasure of running, this is the way to make the most rapid improvements in your performance.

In chapter 10 we shall look at the rationale for running at different speeds, and the implications for putting together a complete training programme. For now, let's just celebrate the great variety of different workouts that runners can do.

Track and interval training

Go down to your local running track on a summer evening and inhale the atmosphere. There is something quite magical about the experience: a wide variety of runners, all confronting the unforgiving certainties of the track. In cities, the track is usually a hive of activity – with runners, throwers and jumpers, and often people playing team sports on the adjacent pitches. There may also be one or two coaches, with whistles and stopwatches, working with their athletes. In smaller communities, there may not be quite so many people at the track, but this is still a good way to meet other runners.

Why do track training?

Speed training is unquestionably the most effective way to improve your running performance. The flat surface and measured distance enable you to see exactly how far, and how fast, you have run. By running faster than your target race pace, you build strength in your muscles, and increase your capacity to produce energy quickly.

Why train at the track?

- performance
- variety
- convenience and time
- concentration
- safety
- motivation
- access to coaching
- enjoyment

Frank Horwill's training squad at the track

Your running form will improve, increasing your efficiency, and you will learn to relax while running fast. Running on the track is also an efficient way to do a hard workout because you compress your effort into a short space of time.

How to do track training

There are infinitely many different sessions you can do on the track. Runners have particular terms to describe different types of track workout. The most common are:

- **sprints**: these flat-out runs mainly improve your running form; **strides** are slower versions of sprints;
- **repetitions** or **repeats**: that is, running fast for a short period, then taking as much time as you need to recover;
- **interval training** (the most common), which is like repetitions except that the focus of the workout is on limiting the rest period ('interval') between each effort; the key to this type of training is that you do not fully recover between efforts.

An interval session is defined by the length of the efforts; the pace at which the efforts are run; then number of efforts; and the time permitted for recovery. So a typical interval session might consist of 6 efforts of 1 mile (4 laps of a 400 m track) at your 10 km race pace; with a rest of 45 seconds between each effort. This is an excellent session for improving your 10 km times.

The sessions you should do depend on your current level of fitness, and your goals. If you plan to run half marathons and marathons, you should probably run longer intervals at a slower pace than if you are training for a 5 km.

Frank Horwill's five-tier pace system

To get the most benefit from track training you need to do a variety of different interval sessions, involving running at a number of different paces. British running coach Frank Horwill has made a key contribution to our understanding of how we should choose our training paces.[44]

Thirty years ago, Frank Horwill invented his *five-tier pace* system, which requires runners to train in different sessions at their 400 m, 800 m, 1500 m, 3 k and 5 k race paces. Horwill established that running at these different paces ensures that the athlete develops both strength and stamina. This approach was adopted (with some success!) by Sebastian Coe, and was used by other members of the British Milers Club, which Horwill founded and which led to Britain's middle distance running heyday of the 1980s.

The five-tier pace system can be adapted for distance runners using a hierarchy of slower paces, such as your 3 km, 5 km, 10 km, half marathon and marathon paces. Table 9.1 will enable you to work out the correct paces for you.

Frank Horwill has a rule of thumb that your pace slows by about 4 seconds a lap for men, or 5 seconds a lap for women, as the race distance increases (i.e. 400 m, 800 m, 1500 m, 3 km, 5 km). For example, if you are a woman whose best time for 800 m is 3:00 (90 seconds

Frank Horwill, founder of the British Milers Club and inventor of multipace training

a lap), then your 1500 m pace should be 95 seconds a lap. In addition, the rest intervals get longer when the pace goes up (see table 9.1 for an example).

It is important to stick firmly to the recovery intervals: if you find that you are unable to keep to the planned session, then slow down the pace of your *efforts* rather than increase the time of the *recovery*.

Table 9.1 Frank Horwill's five-tier pace system

Pace	Time (example 1)	Time (example 2)	Distance	Recovery
5000 m	105 sec/lap	76 sec/lap	4 × 1 mile	60–90 secs
3000 m	100 sec/lap	72 sec/lap	6 × 1000 m	75–120 secs
1500 m	95 sec/lap	68 sec/lap	6 × 600 m	90–120 secs
800 m	90 sec/lap	64 sec/lap	4 × 400 m	120–180 secs
400 m	85 sec/lap	40 sec/lap	8 × 200 m	120–180 secs

Adapted from Frank Horwill, *Obsession for Running*, 1991.

ler Fartlek

ion is named after Wodlemar Gerschler of Germany who developed the
; of interval training during the 1930s. The Gerschler Fartlek is done on the
track, and is good training for getting fit quickly. After a warm-up jog, you stride hard
for 30 seconds, followed by a 90-second jog. You do five more efforts at the same
intensity, but with a 15-second reduction in the recovery each time. So the session is
30/90, 30/75, 30/60, 30/45, 30/30, 30/15. This is repeated three times. At the end, do
a 10-minute warm-down jog.

How often to do track training

In general you should aim to run on the track once or perhaps twice a week if you are
a long distance runner; and up to five times a fortnight if you are a middle distance
runner or shorter. But you should be aware that track training is physically hard, and
the type most likely to lead to injury. So you should build up slowly – you should
certainly not go from nothing to three times a week in one step.

Hills

Hill training is an important part of any runner's repertoire. Hill work is
complementary to strength and speed training.

Why do hill training?

Why is it important to have strong legs? The speed you run depends on two things:
the length of your stride, and your leg turnover (i.e. the number of strides you take
per minute). This is blindingly obvious if you think about it: but it has important
implications. If you increase your stride length, you will run faster. To do this you
need to improve your *flexibility*, but also your leg *strength* so that you push off with
greater power for each step.

For longer distance running, leg strength is also a key factor in developing your
stamina. Hill workouts strengthen your hamstrings, calves and buttocks, but
especially the thigh muscles (*quadriceps*), which don't get much of a workout from
running on the flat. Marathon runners, in particular, need strong quads to sustain
their effort over the full distance.

It is also important to develop leg strength as a way to avoid injury. Before you start
intense speed training, you should have a base of leg strength which gives you the
explosive power you need for speed.

Hill running not only develops stronger legs, it is also character-building. And if
you make hill sessions a regular part of your training, you will find that the hills in
your race slip by (well, almost).

> 'Having had a tough day at work, I came to training this evening feeling
> exhausted and run down. By the end of my workout, I felt as if I could take on
> the world.'
>
> *David Ferrier, runner and theatre manager*

So hill training is valuable for runners of any distance, and especially for half marathons and marathons. You should plan to increase your hill sessions at the beginning of the training cycle, before you start the serious speed work.

How to do a hill session

A typical session involves finding a hill that is anywhere between 200 m and 1 km long, with a gradient of between 5 and 15 per cent. Warm up for ten minutes (you may be able to do this by jogging from home to the hill). Then run up the hill hard, keeping your head up and shoulders back. Emphasise your style: push off your feet, lift your knees, and pump your arms hard. As the gradient of the hill changes, try to hold your effort (not your speed) constant. At the top of the hill, keep running; and jog back down to the bottom and repeat.

If you are new to hill sessions, begin with about a mile of hill running (plus a mile of jogging down again); and gradually build up to three or four miles. The number of repeats will depend on the length of the hill.

An alternative way to build hills into your schedule is to plan one of your longer routes to include a hilly section (if necessary, repeating a loop of the route with a good hill in it). Again, your aim should be to maintain your effort levels as the gradient increases. Try to ensure that you run a total of at least two to three miles uphill with a gradient of at least 7 per cent.

If you are really stuck for hills where you live, you can sometimes improvise, using a treadmill in your gym (which can be set to a gradient); or stairs at home or in the office.

Fartlek

Fartlek literally means 'speed play' in Swedish (the idea was invented by Swedish coach Gusta Holmer). It means the introduction of faster bursts into a slower run.

Why do fartleks?

The purpose of fartlek is to increase your fitness. Fartlek recruits your fast twitch muscle fibres during a longer run, so ensuring that the whole muscle is getting a good workout. Fartlek also helps to build speed and strength.

How to do a fartlek

Fartlek runs can be done as an unstructured session (i.e. running faster as you feel inclined); or in a more structured way (e.g. 10 surges of 400 m). The best place to do fartleks is generally on a trail run or in a park, though some athletes prefer to do them on a track.

A typical fartlek session might be a 10-minute warm-up jog; then hard strides for 3–4 minutes, with 1-minute recoveries, for 10–15 minutes; then a 10-minute jog to cool down.

Another way to do fartleks is to use landmarks, such as lamp-posts or trees. For example, you might decide to run hard for the next eight lamp-posts, and then jog for a minute. Some running clubs organise fartleks in which different runners take it in turns to lead the group, increasing the pace to hard strides periodically as they see fit, while the rest of the group keeps up with them.

Threshold runs

Threshold runs – also known as tempo runs - are often favoured by long distance runners (10 km and over). They involve running at about your anaerobic threshold (also known as your lactate threshold). This is the maximum speed at which your body can work aerobically for long periods (see chapter 10 for more details). It is thought that by training at this level, you can gradually increase the body's capacity to produce energy aerobically and its ability to cope with the build-up of lactic acid. Threshold runs are an excellent way to improve your 10 km race performances.

> 'What doesn't destroy me makes me stronger.'
>
> *Friedrich Nietzsche, Twilight of the Idols.*
> *[Not, apparently, written about threshold runs]*

How to do a threshold run

A threshold run generally consists of a 10-minute warm up, followed by 20–30 minutes of running at just below your anaerobic threshold, followed by 5 minutes of warm-down.

The tricky part is getting the pace right. One way to gauge the pace of your threshold run is to find the pace at which you can *just* hold a conversation. You should be able to talk, but perhaps not in complete sentences. If you are too out of breath to speak at all, you are running too fast. But if you can speak normally, you are running too slowly. You are aiming to run 'comfortably hard'.

If you are an experienced runner, your threshold pace should be somewhere between your 10-mile race pace and your half-marathon race pace, or about 10–30 seconds a mile slower than your 10 km race pace.

Alternatively, you can use a heart rate monitor to ensure that you do your threshold run just below your aerobic threshold. Your aerobic threshold is generally about 70–80 per cent of your working heart rate, or 78–85 per cent of your maximum heart rate (see the next chapter).

The key to threshold runs is to resist the temptation to go too fast. This is deliberately not a maximum effort workout. As you become fitter, these runs should become easier, until you review your threshold pace. You should not go as fast as you can from one week to the next: as you feel stronger, you should try to achieve the same pace and distance with less effort.

Long runs

The long slow distance (LSD) run is the cornerstone of any long distance runner's training programme. (One reason why the term 'LSD run' is so appropriate is that it is one of the most reliable ways of getting the 'runner's high').

Why do long slow distance runs?

The LSD run has many benefits. First, it helps to adapt your joints and muscles to give them the endurance for long runs. Second, it improves your cardiovascular system, strengthens the heart and increases the blood supply in the muscles; it therefore enhances the body's capacity to deliver oxygen to your muscles. Third, it enhances your body's ability to burn fat as a source of energy. Fourth, it teaches your body to store more energy as glycogen in your muscles. And finally, long slow runs teach the body to run efficiently, minimising the energy expenditure needed to move you along. Even if you are not training for a marathon, the long slow distance run is a key element in your overall fitness programme.

How to do long slow distance runs

The LSD run should be run slowly to ensure that you are developing the fat-burning metabolic pathway, and to minimise the effect of fatigue and risk of injury. It should be around 20 per cent slower than your marathon pace; or 25–30 per cent slower than your half-marathon pace. You may be surprised at first how slow this seems. If you use a heart rate monitor, try to keep your heart rate within 60–70 per cent of the working heart rate zone, or 70–78 per cent of your maximal heart rate (see chapter 10).

The distance of the long slow distance run depends on the length of the race for which you are training. For a 5 km race, the LSD need not be more than 5–10 miles; but for marathon runners it needs to be more like 20 miles (or longer for advanced runners). This is discussed in more detail in chapter 10.

For many runners, one morning of each weekend is set aside for the long run; and running clubs often organise Sunday morning long runs. In the run-up to major marathons, such as the London Marathon, there are also lots of organised races of up to 20 miles that you can use for your long runs (though you should resist the temptation to run these too fast). If you are training for a half marathon or marathon you can use your long run to practise some key elements of the big day (see chapter 12 for more information about long runs as part of marathon training).

Rehearsal runs

If you are training for a half marathon or longer, you may want to add a rehearsal run into your training programme.

Why do rehearsal runs?

The inspiration behind this workout is that many runners never actually run at their intended race pace. They run faster on the track, and slower in their long run; but their body has not got used to running at the pace they intend to run. It is useful to adapt the muscles and tendons, as well as the mind, to running at the intended race pace.

How to do rehearsal runs

Frank Horwill recommends beginning your sequence of rehearsal runs about 12 weeks before a marathon.[45] Start with a nine-mile run, at your intended marathon pace. Run it at *exactly* the pace you intend to run the marathon. The following week, increase the distance to 10 miles. If you don't succeed in covering the distance within a couple of minutes of the target time, repeat the distance the following week until you are bang on target. Go on increasing the distance by a mile each week, up to 18 miles (which should be about three weeks before the marathon). Note that this rehearsal run is intended to be *additional* to your long slow run.

This is quite a demanding additional workout during the week, and I would not recommend it for beginners training for a marathon. However, it is sensible for beginners to get some practice at running at their intended marathon pace. One way to do this is to use a weekend race – such as a half marathon – to practise running at marathon pace. Another option is to aim to run the last third (but no more) of your weekly long run at your marathon pace (remember that your long run should normally be about 20 per cent slower than marathon pace). Either way, this will get you some experience of running at your intended pace.

Cross training

To a runner, *cross training* means doing exercise other than running, such as cycling, swimming or working out in the gym. The best exercise to improve your running performance is running; but other exercises can play an important part in your training programme.

Why do cross training?

All exercise will increase or maintain your fitness and provide other physical benefits, but because the body's adaptation to exercise is quite specific, running is the most efficient way to exercise to improve your running performance.

Nonetheless, cross training can play an important role in your training programmes. The main advantages of doing other forms of exercise are that they increase your overall levels of fitness without adding to the repetitive stress of running. Some exercise, such as swimming and dance, can also improve your flexibility, and offset some of the tightness caused by running. Cross training can also help to prevent injuries, by reducing the extent of muscle imbalance, and by replacing running with non-weight-bearing activities, eliminating some of the impact on the ground. Cross training is also a good way to keep fit while doing things that can include non-running partners, children or other special people in your life. You can, for example, go out for a cycle ride with your family.

Many runners switch to cycling or swimming if they have an injury that stops them from running as a way to keep fit, and in pursuit of the endorphin-fuelled 'buzz' of exercise that they would otherwise miss.

There is a rule of thumb that runners may find useful when thinking about cross training. Swimming one mile is roughly 'equivalent' (in terms of energy expenditure and benefits to fitness) to four miles of running; and four miles of running are in turn roughly equivalent to 16 miles of cycling. Table 6.8 shows the energy expenditure for various forms of exercise.

Cross training: weight training

One particular form of cross training merits particular mention: working out in the gym. Bruce Fordyce, the legendary winner of the Comrades ultra-marathon in South Africa, attributes his success in part to his regular gym workouts.

Rugby players run to improve fitness

Weight training can increase the strength and stability of the upper body, which in turn improves running efficiency. It also builds lean muscle, which increases the metabolic rate, reducing fat, and enhances the body's ability to store glycogen.

However, weight training that increases your muscle size increases your weight, which is a handicap for long distance runners. If you are a seriously competitive runner for whom additional weight is likely to influence your performance, you should use weights in a way that increases your strength and muscle tone but not muscle bulk (i.e. do lots of repetitions with light weights).

You don't need to be a member of a gym to do effective strength exercises for your upper or lower body. There are lots of exercises you can do at home, without any special equipment, such as press-ups, sit-ups, leg raises and knee bends.

Easy runs and recovery runs

The **easy run** and **recovery run** are important ingredients in a training programme.

Why do easy runs?

Easy runs are a good way for long distance athletes to build endurance. Shorter and less demanding of time than the long slow distance run, they enable you to put more miles on your legs without tiring yourself out.

A particular form of easy run is the **recovery run**, which follows a hard training session. Some elite athletes who run twice a day will follow a morning track session with an evening recovery run. For the rest of us, a recovery run is usually the day after a hard training session.

The key to training is recovery – your body does not adapt while it is under stress, but afterwards when you are recovering. This recovery and adaptation can be enhanced by gentle exercise, which helps to clear the waste products out of the muscles and increase the blood flow. After a hard session or a long distance run, it is usually better to do a recovery run the following day than to rest completely.

How to do easy runs and recovery runs

Easy runs are typically about 3–6 miles. (Recovery runs should be at the smaller end of this range, lasting around 20–30 minutes.) They should be shorter and faster than a long slow distance run. For experienced runners, they are run at about your marathon pace, or a bit slower. The pace should feel comfortable and you should be able to talk in full sentences easily.

The main risk with recovery runs is that you will run too hard, and so give your body insufficient opportunity to recover. You may want to leave your watch at home, so that you are not tempted to push yourself too much.

Rest

Probably the most important ingredient in the training cookbook is rest. It is when you are resting that the body rebuilds muscles and joints, and adapts to the demands it has to meet.

As you increase your running, you are likely to need more sleep. When you are training hard, reckon on **an extra hour a night of sleep**, especially if you are currently getting less than seven hours a night. This extra sleep is a considerable time commitment on top of the time you spend running, and needs to be taken into account when deciding how much training is feasible for you, given the other things you want to do.

Apart from extra sleep, you need to make sure that you are getting enough rest between hard sessions. Never do hard training sessions (e.g. intervals, hills or threshold runs) on consecutive days – you need a day in between to recover.

Over longer time horizons, as we shall see in the next chapter, you should aim to have an **easy week once a month**, in which you cut back your training volumes. You should also aim to have an **easy month once a year** in which you switch to other exercises such as swimming and cycling, and either don't run at all or run only gently, as you feel inclined, without a watch.

Conclusion

Runners are blessed with a huge variety of choices – from the short, hard efforts of interval training, to the long, languid weekend runs so beloved of marathon runners. Using all these different workouts adds variety and interest to your running, and enables you to fit your running into your lifestyle. And if you want to get from 'hobby jogging' to more serious running, you are going to need to use a mixture of these techniques to improve your performance. The next chapter will show you how.

10 Training cookbook: putting it together

We have looked at the different ingredients that you can use in your training programme. This chapter is about putting them together.

A training programme is going to be effective and sustained only if it is designed around your ability, goals, and other commitments. If you had your own coach, you could work with him or her to design a programme tailored for you. This chapter will help you to be your own coach, and enable you to design a training programme that suits you, rather than rely on an 'over the counter' training programme that may not suit your needs.

Most of this chapter is written on the assumption that you are training for a race. You don't have to be an elite athlete to take part in races, and lots of runners take part in races just to enjoy the atmosphere and measure their performance and progress against their goals. But even if you are not training for a race, you can use the same principles to improve your fitness and your running performance.

Training programme principles

- Train at different paces.
- Make every session count.
- Include enough rest.
- Don't do consecutive hard sessions.
- Ease back one week a month.
- Take one month a year off.

Why it is important to run at different speeds

Training makes you a better runner by causing controlled physical stress, which in turn leads to adaptation of the body. Different types of training stress the body in different ways, and so lead to different types of adaptation. So you need to do a combination of types of training so that all the components of your running performance are improved.

The determinants of running performance

The various components of running that you will improve by training are:

- the **cardiovascular system**; this provides oxygen to the muscles, improvements include strengthening the heart to enable it to pump more blood, and improving the amount of oxygen carried by the blood;
- your **running muscles**; improvements include increasing the number and size of your mitochondria (which are the places within your muscle cells where aerobic metabolism actually takes place); increasing the blood supply within the muscle,

which brings fuel and oxygen in and takes waste products away; improving the ability of the muscles to store glycogen; and increasing the strength, stamina and flexibility of the muscles;

- your **metabolic system**, which converts carbohydrate, fat and protein into energy; this can adapt to be more efficient at converting fat into energy, enabling long distance runners to go for longer before they 'hit the wall';
- your **joints, ligaments and bones**, which adapt to running, increasing their strength and elasticity and your resilience and resistance to injury;
- your **running technique**, which determines your efficiency in translating muscular output into movement.

As we shall see later in the chapter, there are five different training paces that you need to include in your training programme to get the biggest impact on all the different determinants of running performance.

> 'When I was younger, running increased mileage led to improved performance. Frustratingly, after I turned 40 I found that running additional miles did not lead to faster times. And anyway, my other commitments did not permit me to run ever-increasing mileage. I started training on the five-tier pace system after the 2000 Boston Marathon. In the following 12 months, I ran fewer miles per week and set new personal best times for the 5 k, ½ marathon and the marathon.'
>
> *Phil McCubbins, Hawaii Ironman Finisher, 1990*

Training zones

In order to put together a training programme, we need to divide our running into different running intensities. Each intensity is aimed at stressing the body in a different way, and hence leads to a different kind of adaptation. These different exercise intensities are often called 'training zones'.

Confusingly, there are three different (but related) tools that are commonly used to define training zones:

- you can define your exercise intensity as a **percentage of VO$_2$ max** – that is, as a proportion of maximum capacity to turn oxygen into energy (see below); for example, easy running is 65–75 per cent of VO$_2$ max; and your threshold run effort level is about 80–90 per cent of VO$_2$ max;
- you can define intensity according to your **heart rate**; because of the availability of relatively cheap heart rate monitors, this is a convenient way to specify different levels of exertion. The relationship between percentage of working heart rate and percentage of VO$_2$ max is complicated, as we shall see;
- you can judge your exercise intensity by considering the **pace** you are running; for example, the easy running zone is slower than marathon race pace; the threshold zone is about your half marathon race pace.

Personally, I reckon the most useful way to define and monitor training intensity is to use *pace*. This seems to me to be both convenient and to have the strongest scientific and empirical underpinning. But since there are lots of runners who use

VO_2 max or heart rates to describe their running intensity, we shall look at all three, and show how they fit together.

Using VO_2 max

One approach to training, which is used by many elite athletes, is to base your training zones on a measure of the body's ability to use oxygen to generate energy.

What is VO_2 max?

As you increase your effort when you exercise, the amount of oxygen you consume to produce energy (and hence the rate at which you exhale carbon dioxide) increases. However, there is a maximum level of oxygen consumption, beyond which increases in exercise intensity don't lead to further increases in oxygen consumption. This level of oxygen consumption is called the VO_2 max. (The initials simply stand for volume of oxygen.)

Some experts believe that VO_2 max is a key physiological determinant of an athlete's running performance, and that it is an important objective of a training programme to improve it. Other sports scientists argue that the limits to an athlete's running performance are determined by a range of factors – such as adaptation of muscles, running efficiency, metabolism – and that VO_2 max is simply a measure of the oxygen that the athlete consumes at the maximum level of energy output. On this view, which I find persuasive, VO_2 max is not the critical factor that determines maximum performance, but is rather a consequence of a combination of other limiting factors. Whichever way you look at it there is a measurable level of exercise intensity at which the athlete's consumption of oxygen reaches a plateau and does not increase further, which we call VO_2 max.

How to measure VO_2 max

To measure VO_2 max accurately, the athlete has to exercise in a laboratory (for example, on a treadmill or exercise bike) to the point of exhaustion. At the point when the athlete is working at peak power output, a sample of exhaled air is captured for analysis. The amount of carbon dioxide in the sample provides a measure of the amount of oxygen the athlete is burning (that is, converting into energy) at maximum energy output – which is the athlete's VO_2 max.

All this involves a gas analysis by a laboratory. Fortunately, there are a number of less complicated ways of approximating the measurement of VO_2 max. These involve measuring an athlete's performance (e.g. how far they can run in fifteen minutes) and then using known correlations to predict the VO_2 max. When done properly, these approximations are good predictors of an accurately measured VO_2 max.

The two most common tests for VO_2 max are the **Balke Test**, described in the box, and the **Bleep Test**, which involves running backwards and forwards between two lines 20 m apart, getting faster and faster, until the athlete is unable to reach the other line. Both tests are *maximal* in that they involve testing the athlete to exhaustion (i.e. beyond the exercise intensity of VO_2 max). Alternative measures of VO_2 max (often used in high-street gyms) work by extrapolating from sub-maximal performances; these are less reliable.

The Balke Test of VO_2 max

Bruno Balke's test to predict VO_2 max is accurate to within ± 5%.

The athlete runs around a track for exactly 15 minutes: the aim is to cover the maximum possible distance. (Athletes should be advised to hold back a little for the first five minutes; to run hard for the next five; and to go full out for the last five.)

Record the total distance run in 15 minutes. To convert the distance covered into VO_2 max, you use the following formula:

VO_2 max = (Metres run × 0.0115) + 10.4

Example results: Distance (m)	VO_2 max
2500	39.1
3000	44.9
3500	50.6
4000	56.4
4500	62.1
5000	67.9

Your VO_2 max is to a large extent determined by your genes; but it can be increased by training. Most people can increase their VO_2 max by between 5 and 20 per cent (increases of up to 60 per cent have been reported); but there is a small proportion of the population for whom training seems to make little difference.

Table 10.1 Measured VO_2 max of elite athletes [46]

Athlete	Performance	VO_2 max
John Ngugi	5 × world cross-country champ	85.0
Dave Bedford	10 km WR 1973	85.0
Steve Prefontaine	1 mile in 3:54.6	84.4
Joan Benoit	2:24:52 marathon	78.6
Bill Rodgers	2:09:27 marathon	78.5
Sebastian Coe	1 mile WR	77.0
Grete Waitz	Marathon WR 1980	73.0
Derek Clayton	Marathon WR 1969	69.7

VO$_2$ max and training zones

Having established the VO$_2$ max as the maximum rate at which the body can consume oxygen, the various other levels of exercise intensity can be defined in relation to this maximum. In a very influential book, *Daniels' Running Formula*, Jack Daniels[47] defines the main training zones as follows:

Table 10.2 Training Zones

Intensity	% VO$_2$ max
Repeats	> 100
Interval training	98–100
Anaerobic threshold	86–88
Easy run/LSD	65–75

But this rather begs the question of how we can use this information in practice. While some of us have measured our VO$_2$ max, few of us have any reliable way of measuring our oxygen consumption as we run, nor do we have a reliable way of knowing what our oxygen consumption is at a given pace. So we need some way to relate our actual exercise intensity while we are running to these target training intensities. In the absence of measurements of our own individual oxygen consumption at different levels of exercise, we have to use approximations, based on tables that relate training paces to proportions of VO$_2$ max. The following table, from *Daniels' Running Formula*, is a good example.

Table 10.3 Training intensities based on current VO$_2$ max

VO$_2$ max	Long, slow distance		Marathon	Threshold pace			Interval pace			Repeats		
	1 km	1 mile	1 mile	400 m	1 km	1 mile	400 m	1 km	1 mile	200 m	400 m	800 m
30	7:37	12:16	11:02	2:33	6:24	10:18	2:22	–	–	67	2:16	–
32	7:16	11:41	10:29	2:26	6:05	9:47	2:14	–	–	63	2:08	–
34	6:56	11:09	10:00	2:19	5:48	9:20	2:08	–	–	60	2:02	–
36	6:38	10:40	9:33	2:13	5:33	8:55	2:02	5:07	–	57	1:55	–
38	6:22	10:14	9:08	2:07	5:19	8:33	1:56	4:54	–	54	1:50	–
40	6:07	9:50	8:46	2:02	5:06	8:12	1:52	4:42	–	52	1:46	–
42	5:53	9:28	8:25	1:57	4:54	7:52	1:48	4:31	–	50	1:42	–
44	5:40	9:07	8:06	1:53	4:43	7:33	1:44	4:21	–	48	98	–
45	5:34	8:58	7:57	1:51	4:38	7:25	1:42	4:16	–	47	96	–
46	5:28	8:48	7:48	1:49	4:33	7:17	1:40	4:12	–	46	94	–
47	5:23	8:39	7:40	1:47	4:29	7:10	98	4:07	–	45	92	–

Table 10.3 continued...

VO$_2$ max	Long, slow distance		Mara-thon	Threshold pace			Interval pace			Repeats		
	1 km	1 mile	1 mile	400 m	1 km	1 mile	400 m	1 km	1 mile	200 m	400 m	800 m
48	5:17	8:31	7:32	1:45	4:24	7:02	96	4:03	–	44	90	–
49	5:12	8:22	7:24	1:43	4:20	6:55	95	3:59	–	44	89	–
50	5:07	8:14	7:17	1:42	4:15	6:51	93	3:55	–	43	87	–
51	5:02	8:07	7:09	1:40	4:11	6:44	92	3:51	–	42	86	–
52	4:58	7:59	7:02	98	4:07	6:38	91	3:48	–	42	85	–
53	4:53	7:52	6:56	97	4:04	6:32	90	3:44	–	41	84	–
54	4:49	7:45	6:49	95	4:00	6:26	88	3:41	–	40	82	–
55	4:45	7:38	6:43	94	3:56	6:20	87	3:37	–	40	81	–
56	4:40	7:31	6:37	93	3:53	6:15	86	3:34	–	39	80	–
57	4:36	7:25	6:31	91	3:50	6:09	85	3:31	–	39	79	
58	4:33	7:19	6:25	90	3:45	6:04	83	3:28	–	38	77	–
59	4:29	7:13	6:19	89	3:43	5:59	82	3:25	–	37	76	–
60	4:25	7:07	6:14	88	3:40	5:54	81	3:23	–	37	75	2:30
61	4:22	7:01	6:09	86	3:37	5:50	80	3:20	–	36	74	2:28
62	4:18	6:56	6:04	85	3:34	5:45	79	3:17	–	36	73	2:26
63	4:15	6:50	5:59	84	3:32	5:41	78	3:15	–	35	72	2:24
64	4:12	6:45	5:54	83	3:29	5:36	77	3:12	–	35	71	2:22
65	4:09	6:40	5:49	82	3:26	5:32	76	3:10	–	34	70	2:20
66	4:05	6:35	5:45	81	3:24	5:28	75	3:08	5:00	34	69	2:18
67	4:02	6:30	5:40	80	3:21	5:24	74	3:05	4:57	33	68	2:16
68	4:00	6:26	5:36	79	3:19	5:20	73	3:03	4:53	33	67	2:14
69	3:57	6:21	5:32	78	3:16	5:16	72	3:01	4:50	32	66	2:12
70	3:54	6:17	5:28	77	3:14	5:13	71	2:59	4:46	32	65	2:10
71	3:51	6:12	5:24	76	3:12	5:09	70	2:57	4:43	31	64	2:08
72	3:49	6:08	5:20	76	3:10	5:05	69	2:55	4:40	31	63	2:06
73	3:46	6:04	5:16	75	3:08	5:02	69	2:53	4:37	31	62	2:05
74	3:44	6:00	5:12	74	3:06	4:59	68	2:51	4:34	30	62	2:04
75	3:41	5:56	5:09	74	3:04	4:56	67	2:49	4:31	30	61	2:03
76	3:39	5:52	5:05	73	3:02	4:52	66	2:48	4:28	29	60	2:02
77	3:36	5:48	5:01	72	3:00	4:49	65	2:46	4:25	29	59	2:00
78	3:34	5:45	4:58	71	2:58	4:46	65	2:44	4:23	29	59	1:59

Table 10.3 continued...

VO$_2$ max	Long, slow distance		Marathon	Threshold pace			Interval pace			Repeats		
	1 km	1 mile	1 mile	400 m	1 km	1 mile	400 m	1 km	1 mile	200 m	400 m	800 m
79	3:32	5:41	4:55	70	2:56	4:43	64	2:42	4:20	28	58	1:58
80	3:30	5:38	4:52	70	2:54	4:41	64	2:41	4:17	28	58	1:56
81	3:28	5:34	4:49	69	2:53	4:38	63	2:39	4:15	28	57	1:55
82	3:26	5:31	4:46	68	2:51	4:35	62	2:38	4:12	27	56	1:54
83	3:24	5:28	4:43	68	2:49	4:32	62	2:36	4:10	27	56	1:53
84	3:22	5:25	4:40	67	2:48	4:30	61	2:35	4:08	27	55	1:52
85	3:20	5:21	4:37	66	2:46	4:27	61	2:33	4:05	27	55	1:51

Adapted from Jack Daniels, *Daniels' Running Formula*, 1998.

Training with heart rate information

As exercise intensity increases, so does your heart rate. Your heart rate, which is conventionally measured in beats per minute (bpm) can therefore be used as an indicator of exercise intensity. Heart rate monitors are available for £50 or more – see chapter 3 for more details.

Determining your maximum heart rate

Unlike your resting heart rate, which falls as you get fitter, your maximum heart rate does not vary much with fitness. It does fall as you get older.

Rules of thumb for estimating your maximum heart rate based on your age are shown in the box. But be aware that these are very rough estimates, and each individual's maximum heart rate might be quite different from the estimate provided by this formula (in some cases, the formula is out by more than 20 beats a minute). The formula is therefore not particularly useful, except as an extremely imprecise estimate.

How to predict your maximum heart rate

Men: MHR $= 214 - (0.8 \times \text{age})$ Women: MHR $= 209 - (0.9 \times \text{age})$

The best way to test your maximum heart rate is to do a running test which you can do on a track, in a park or on a treadmill. After warming up, run at an even pace for three minutes, as fast as you can. Jog for two minutes, then run again for three minutes as fast as you can. Your maximum heart rate is the maximum level reached during the second three-minute run.

If you are significantly overweight, however, you should seek medical advice before you undertake a maximal heart rate test of this kind.

Resting heart rate

The best way to measure your resting heart rate is to use a watch or a heart rate monitor before you get out of bed in the morning (and before your first cup of coffee, since caffeine stimulates the heart rate). Some athletes even sleep with their heart rate monitor strapped on!

As you get fitter, your resting heart rate should gradually reduce. If you notice a blip up in your resting heart rate one morning, this is a sign of overtraining or impending illness. (As described in chapter 8, you can also use the increase in your heart rate when you get out of bed as a good early warning indicator of overtraining.)

Using the heart rate to estimate exercise intensity

Heart rates are often used to define and monitor training zones. For example, the low intensity zone or 'fat burning zone' is usually defined as 60–70 per cent of maximum heart rate, and the 'threshold zone' is said to be 80–90 per cent of maximum heart rate.

You can base your training zones either on a percentage of your *maximum* heart rate or on a percentage of your *working* heart rate. Your working heart rate is the zone between your resting heart rate and your maximum heart rate. For example, my maximum heart rate is 190 bpm (four beats a minute higher than the rule of thumb based on my age predicts); and my resting heart rate is 50 bpm. This means my working heart rate is:

WHR – 190 – 50 = 140 bpm.

To get the heart rate corresponding to the anaerobic threshold, which is at 90 per cent of my working heart rate, I have to add 85 per cent of my working heart rate to my resting heart rate. So the heart rate corresponding to my aerobic threshold is estimated to be:

AT = 50 + (0.90 × 140) = 176.

However, for most runners, the heart rate is not an especially good way to calibrate effort. There are many factors that affect the heart rate, including your level of dehydration, temperature, blood sugar, illness and excitement (e.g. adrenalin on race day). Because the heart rate depends on all these factors it is an unreliable guide to your intensity of effort.

However, heart rate measurements can be useful as a proxy for intensity if you know your body well, and you know how your heart rate responds to different conditions. Your heart rate monitor may be especially useful if you don't have reliable information about your pace. It is also useful for monitoring trends in your fitness over time.

Comparing different measures of intensity

We have seen that we can judge running intensity by percentage of VO_2 max, percentage of working heart rate, or by pace. The trouble with using percentage of VO_2 max to regulate our training intensity is that we don't have any direct way of checking our oxygen consumption; so day-to-day we have to fall back on pace or heart rate as a proxy measure to enable us to estimate our oxygen uptake. Nonetheless, many training guides are calibrated on the basis of percentage of VO_2 max.

We can measure heart rates directly, cheaply and while we are running, so this might be a more valuable tool for assessing training intensity. But heart rates can vary quite considerably depending on a variety of conditions, and so they are not an especially good guide to actual exercise intensity on a particular day.

For these reasons, I believe that the simplest and most logical way to judge exercise intensity is to look at the pace. This can also be measured directly (for example, using electronic pedometers described in chapter 3, or by running on a track), and appears to be a good indicator of exercise intensity.

The following table gives an approximate guide to correlation between the different levels of VO$_2$ max, the percent of working heart rate, and the corresponding race pace.

Table 10.4 Comparison of heart rate, VO$_2$ max and race pace

Training zone	Equivalent race pace	% Maximum heart rate	% Working heart rate	% VO$_2$ max
Maximum	400 m	100	100	> 100
VO$_2$ max	3 km	96	94	100
Interval pace	5 km	94	92	98
Anaerobic threshold or lactate threshold	half marathon to 10 mile	85–92	89–90	80–90
Aerobic threshold	marathon, or slower	78–85	70–80	70–80
Long, slow distance	20% slower than marathon	70–78	60–70	60–70

Relationship between maximum heart rate and VO$_2$ max

Your VO$_2$ max generally occurs at between 95 and 98 per cent of your maximum heart rate, so your maximum heart rate is at a higher level of effort than VO$_2$ max. You may be wondering how it is possible that you can exercise at a higher intensity than your VO$_2$ max. Recall that your VO$_2$ max is the most rapid rate at which you can convert oxygen into energy. But very high intensity exercise (such as sprinting) is sustained by anaerobic metabolism – that is, without oxygen. For short periods, your body can produce energy at a higher rate than you can burn oxygen. That is why your maximum energy output can exceed your VO$_2$ max.

The aerobic and anaerobic thresholds

What is the aerobic threshold?

Recall from chapter 7 that the body has different ways to produce energy. The *aerobic* energy system uses oxygen, and burns carbohydrate, fats and proteins. It is relatively slow at producing energy, and therefore cannot be used when a lot of energy is needed quickly. It is, however, the main energy system used for long distance running. For more intensive activity, the body uses *anaerobic* energy systems, which don't require oxygen but which rapidly result in waste products (notably lactic acid and protons) that build up in the muscles and use up limited stores of glycogen.

The *aerobic threshold* is the level of effort at which anaerobic energy pathways start to be a significant part of energy production. Runners want to increase their aerobic threshold because this will enable them to run faster for longer before they tip into anaerobic metabolism, which cannot be sustained for as long.

The pace that corresponds to your aerobic threshold is generally around your marathon pace. This is about 70 per cent of VO_2 max, or about 75 per cent of your working heart rate.

What is the anaerobic threshold?

The *anaerobic threshold* is defined as the level of exercise intensity at which lactic acid builds up in the body faster than it can be cleared away. For this reason it is also sometimes called the *lactate threshold* or *lactate turnpoint*.

There is some controversy (see Noakes, *Lore of Running*) about whether there really is a level of exercise intensity at which lactic acid in the bloodstream begins to increase. There is evidence that lactic acid levels increase smoothly as exercise becomes more intense, and there does not appear to be an identifiable discontinuity or kink in the curve. On this view, the anaerobic threshold is simply the point at which the lactic acid accumulation becomes noticeable to the athlete.

When you run at close to your anaerobic threshold, running should be hard but not uncomfortable. Some runners observe a change in their breathing rhythm at the anaerobic threshold, from one breath for every four steps to one breath for every two steps. At this level of exercise you can continue to speak, but not in complete sentences.

For experienced runners, your anaerobic threshold is somewhere between your half-marathon pace and your 10-mile race pace. It should be about 10–30 seconds a mile slower than your 10 km race pace.

Components of the training week

To maximise your running performance, you need to do training that will improve all the determinants of running performance, and that means doing a variety of different types of workout. In general, your training programme should include a combination of the following five items:[48]

- **long slow distance running (LSD)** – this enhances the metabolism of fat; strengthens the heart, enabling it to pump more blood; increases muscle fuel storage; promotes adaptation of your joints and connective tissues; and increases running efficiency and endurance; LSD running is done at roughly 60–70 per cent of working heart rate, which is about 20 per cent slower than marathon race pace, about once a week;
- **easy running** – easy running also promotes adaptation of joints and connective tissues, and increases endurance; following hard workouts, easy running can accelerate recovery by increasing blood flow; easy runs are done at about 70–80 per cent of working heart rate – a bit slower than your marathon pace; the bulk of your running mileage will be done at this speed;

- **threshold pace** – running at a pace just below your anaerobic threshold: increases your muscle mitochondria, improving your aerobic energy production; increases the blood supply within the muscles; increases blood volume and the oxygenation of the blood; improves stamina; enhances the body's capacity to get rid of and accommodate lactic acid: threshold pace is about 88 per cent of working heart rate; it is a bit faster than your half marathon race pace, or 10–30 seconds a mile slower than your 10 km race pace; your threshold pace runs will last about 20–30 minutes;

- **speed training** – this pushes your cardiovascular system to the limit; it improves your heart's stroke volume (i.e. the amount of blood pushed with each heartbeat); increases the blood supply to your muscles; enhances muscular strength; and improves running form and efficiency, so that you can cover more distance for the same amount of energy expended; speed training is done at 90–100 per cent of working heart rate, or roughly 800 m to 5 km race pace); you will usually do speed sessions on the track; speed work should make up no more than 10 per cent of your weekly training distance; beginners should limit themselves to one interval session per week and experienced runners to two a week or, at most, five per fortnight;

- **rest** – the most important component of the training programme, since this is the time when the body can adapt, in response to the stress of training, and make the repairs that will improve your performance.

These different types of training all produce benefits for all runners, from sprinters to ultra-marathoners. But the right combination of these training techniques will very much depend on your own goals.

As well as improving your running, varying your training in this way reduces the risk that you will get stuck in a rut, and eventually get bored of your running; it also reduces the likelihood of injury and provides options for doing good workouts even when time is short.

> 'Make your plans sustainable. Far better to jog 10 miles a week for life than 60 miles a week for a few months and then give up due to boredom or injury.'
>
> *David Knight, 2:45 marathon runner and photographer for this book*

Should I always run as hard as I can?

There will be times when you feel that you can do a workout faster than the specified pace. But running harder will not necessarily be more effective training, or make you a better runner. The point of training at different paces is to stress the body in various ways, and thus cause a variety of different, complementary adaptations of your body. If you want to improve your aerobic system then doing fast, anaerobic training is not going to help you to improve as much as running at your anaerobic threshold. Apart from the risk of fatigue and injury of making every workout hard, you need to train at different paces to get the maximum all-round improvement.

Training for fitness

Some runners are not particularly interested in improving their running performance. For them, the goals of running are primarily to keep fit, lose weight, and reduce stress rather than training to get faster.

If you have no racing goals, it is still useful to train at different paces to get the best effect of your running on your fitness, because different levels of effort develop your body in different ways.

A programme for all-round fitness should therefore ideally include long slow distance runs, threshold runs, strength training, fartleks, and speed training. As well as providing holistic improvements in your physical fitness, this variety will help to maintain your interest in running and reduce the risk of injury.

To maintain a good level of fitness, you should run four to five times a week for at least half an hour. If you are designing a training schedule for overall fitness, the 10 km and half marathon schedules should be your benchmarks. These include plenty of aerobic running, including workouts near the anaerobic threshold. Avoid hard sessions on two consecutive days, since this increases the risk of injury.

It can be difficult to sustain a training programme of this kind, at least at first, if you don't have a specific goal in mind. If you don't want to take part in a race (see chapter 11) then you might want to set yourself a different, measurable goal. For example, you might want to measure your progress by the fall in your resting heart rate, or by taking a VO_2 max test once every three or four months to see how you are getting on.

How many miles should I run?

There is probably no greater topic of controversy among runners than the ideal mileage.

As far as we know, aerobic capacity does not improve if you run more than 50 miles a week. So if you are interested only in increasing your fitness, this is probably the maximum mileage you need to run. You can, of course, maintain a good level of fitness on much less.

Running performance can continue to improve beyond 50 miles a week, however, even though aerobic conditioning does not. The benefits of big mileage include improvements in the runner's ability to burn fat, increased muscular endurance and maintenance of body weight. The upper limit for physiologically useful increases in mileage appears to be around 80–100 miles a week; though many elite athletes run 100–120 miles a week.

Most runners don't run anything like this sort of distance each week. Clearly, a number of factors affect the optimum mileage:

- **lifestyle constraints**, such as family and work commitments, and other leisure activities;
- the distances, if any, at which we want to **compete** (marathon runners need a higher weekly mileage than 5 km runners);
- our **capacity to train** before we get injured or ill; this is greatly affected by how we train, but there are also some inherited differences.

Here is a table setting out a rough guide of recommended mileages for runners of different experience at different race distances. The judgement you make about weekly mileages will depend on your own circumstances.

Table 10.5 Recommended maximum weekly distances[49] (miles)

Race distance	Beginner	Intermediate	Advanced
5 km	10–20	15–25	30–40
10 km	15–25	20–30	30–50
Half marathon	20–30	25–35	35–50
Marathon	30–40	40–50	40–60

You don't need to run these distances all year round: these are weekly averages in the peak weeks before your race. You should take regular breaks during the year – reducing your mileage, and then build up again.

If your goal is simply to keep fit, then you should be aiming for about 30 miles a week.

How rapidly to increase your mileage

You should not increase your weekly mileage too rapidly if you want to avoid injury or illness. A good rule of thumb is that below 20 miles a week you should not increase your weekly mileage by more than two miles a week; above 20 miles a week, you should not increase your weekly mileage by more than 10 per cent a week. So if you are currently running 10 miles a week, you should not increase to more than 12 miles next week; and if you are running 35 miles a week, you should not increase to more than 38½ miles the next week.

This is a very important guideline. All experience shows that excessively rapid build-up in training mileage is one of the most common causes of injury. Many new runners think that they can be the exception to the rule, because they feel they can go further than this. Sadly, this enthusiasm often ends in tears.

How many times a week to run

If running is your main exercise, you should aim to run three or four times a week, in order to reap the full health benefits (see chapter 1). But runners who set themselves more demanding performance goals will need to run five or six days a week, giving themselves one or two rest days.

Elite runners will often run twice a day on at least some days of the week. For example, they may do a track session in the morning, and a recovery run in the evening. These runners may therefore run 10–12 times a week. Even elite runners generally take one day a week off completely, but some rest only one day a fortnight.

Running twice a day can have advantages if you are trying to do a big weekly mileage, since it seems to be less draining to run two 6-mile runs than one 12-mile run in a day. But remember that there are time overheads, such as the time it takes to change, shower and recover, which you will have to accommodate twice. You should also take into account the effect on your family life of running twice a day. All in all, it is physically demanding to run twice a day, and you should not contemplate it until you have been running for a few years.

The length of the long run

A cornerstone of the running week for many runners is the long run, especially for runners focusing on distances more than 1500 m. The length will vary according to the distance you want to race. Endurance runners will typically do one long run a week; shorter distance runners may do one long run a fortnight.

The long run should, in most cases, be between one-quarter and one-third (certainly less than half) of your weekly mileage. So if you are running 10 miles a week, your long run should be around three to four miles. Your long run should not exceed 18–22 miles.

Table 10.6 sets out recommended distances for long runs. These are the peak distances for your long run during your training schedule, which you will build up to.

Finishing a 20 mile race

Table 10.6 Long run distances[50] (miles)

Race distance	Beginner	Intermediate	Advanced
5 km	3–6	5–8	8–12
10 km	5–8	6–10	10–15
Half marathon	10–13	11–15	13–20
Marathon	18–20	18–20	18–22

Training phases

The mix of training you do each week depends on your goals, your experience and your abilities. But the mix will not be the same all the time: it evolves over time in the build-up to your target race. A simple training programme can be built up using four distinct phases:

- **Base** – Every programme needs a solid foundation of aerobic fitness and endurance. During the base period, you build up to about three-quarters of your peak weekly mileage and long run distance while concentrating on aerobic running. This phase typically lasts from four to eight weeks. During the end of the base phase, runners may start to include some light hill training, fartlek and threshold runs.
- **Strength** – In the next phase, you add hill training, and if necessary leg strength training in the gym, to build up strength and reduce the risk of injury. In this phase you begin to increase the threshold run and fartlek training. This phase lasts two to four weeks.
- **Speed** – The focus then shifts to speed sessions, including one or two interval training sessions each week, while maintaining your threshold runs; if necessary, you may cut back a little on aerobic running. Beginners should beware of doing too much speed work at first because of the risk of injury. This phase lasts three to six weeks.
- **Peaking and tapering for racing** – During this period, you reduce training volume, but maintain the quality of running (for example, by maintaining the same speed but running shorter distances). The length of the taper varies from a few days for a 5 km to three weeks for a marathon (see chapter 11). The peaking phase for shorter distances can last for three to six weeks, during which time you may race several times before the intensity and stress of racing takes its toll.

Note that while these training phases are not wholly distinct, there should be a clearly recognisable change in balance in your training over time.

The following table shows roughly how long each phase should last.

Table 10.7 Approximate length in weeks of training phases

Phase	5 km	10 km	Half	Marathon
Base	4–6	4–6	5–8	6–8
Strength	2–4	2–4	3–5	3–6
Speed	3–4	3–4	3–6	3–6
Peak	3–6	3–6	2-week taper	3-week taper
Total	12–20	12–20	13–21	15–23

Easy weeks

Most runners benefit from cutting back for an easy week, one week in four. In these weeks, the runner should reduce the mileage to about 75 per cent of normal weekly mileage, while maintaining the speed and quality of the sessions. These easy weeks give your body a chance to recover. If you try to train continuously for more than 12 weeks without some respite, the chances are that you will get ill or injured. It is much better to plan to take an easy week than have one forced upon you.

Putting it together

We now have all the ingredients in place so that we can put together our own training programme.

Mapping out the weeks

You need to figure out how many weeks you are going to need, and how your programme will be phased over those weeks.

The **first step** is to decide your **goal**. This determines the amount of mileage and type of training you need to do. Your goal should be stretching but achievable. You should reassess, and if necessary adjust, your goal as your training progresses. (See chapter 2 for more about setting a goal.)

Second, determine your **desired weekly mileage**, using Table 10.5. Consider carefully how much time you are prepared to commit to running, and take account of the impact on your family and social life. Don't forget that as you increase your exercise, you should also increase the amount of sleep you get, which you will also need to budget for.

Third, calculate how long it will take you to **build up to your desired weekly mileage**, given that you should not increase your weekly mileage by more than two miles, or 10 per cent a week, whichever is the larger. (If you follow this strictly, it takes around three months to get from 10 to 40 miles a week.)

Fourth, decide the **total duration of the training programme**, remembering to include the time it will take to build up to your desired weekly mileage. In the light of the duration, select your target race or races.

Now you can draw up your **training overview**, showing all the weeks between now and the target race date, which forms the basis of your plan. Write in the training goals for each week, identify the easy weeks, and pencil in approximate weekly mileage totals.

Table 10.8 Sample training overview for 10 km runner

Weeks to go	Phase	Miles	Weeks to go	Phase	Miles
22	Build up	10	11	Base	20
21	Build up	12	10	Strength	22
20	Build up	8 E	9	Strength	24
19	Build up	12	8	Strength	16 E
18	Build up	14	7	Speed	25
17	Build up	16	6	Speed	23
16	Base	10 E	5	Speed	25
15	Base	16	4	Speed	16 E
14	Base	18	3	Speed	22
13	Base	20	2	Peaking	20
12	Base	16 E	1	Race	15

E denotes easy week

Table 10.8 gives an example for a runner who runs 10 miles a week, wants to run a 10 km, and has decided to step up to 25 miles a week. The schedule therefore begins with 12 weeks of aerobic running, building up to the target weekly mileage of 25 miles a week.

Designing the weekly programme in detail

Once you have the overall shape of the programme, you can then begin to fill in planned run details for each day of the week. How you do this will depend on your other commitments, and factors (for example, if you are a member of a running club, the weekly timetable of your club runs).

The first step is to write in your weekly **long run**. This should build up to your maximum long run, which you should repeat each fortnight three or four times. Your longest run should be three to four weeks before the race. In easy weeks, cut back the long run to around two-thirds of the previous week.

Then pencil in your **rest days**. You may want to rest on Fridays, so that you are strong for weekend races; or on Mondays after the rigours of the weekend.

Then pencil in your **strength sessions, speed sessions**, and **threshold runs**. Ideally, these should be separated from each other, and from your long runs, by at least a day (though sometimes this is impossible).

The training schedules in chapter 11 give examples of how your programme might look.

How detailed should your schedule be?

Some runners prefer to plan every session in advance. Others prefer to leave things open, so that they can adapt their training to unexpected work or social commitments and how their body feels.

An approach that seems to work well for many runners is to map out an overview of the training programme, and pencil in weekly mileage totals. Then write in any fixed points, such as races you want to enter, long runs and weekly club runs. This gives the programme a skeleton. But you might want to leave the rest vague: for example, you could decide not to schedule easy runs, fartleks, threshold runs and rest days, and run these sessions as you feel inclined. All the while, use your training log to keep an eye on your weekly mileage to make sure it is in line with the target you have set yourself.

What if you miss a training session?

We all miss the occasional training session. Do not catch up by fitting in back-to-back hard sessions, or by increasing your mileage on other days. Just continue your training schedule as before.

Varying your training over the year

We have seen that the training schedule in the run-up to a race should move through different training phases, from aerobic base, to strength and then speed. In addition, most serious runners vary their training patterns over the year.

For example, some runners spend the winter months concentrating on building distance and endurance, using the dark evenings for long runs; taking part in cross-country races; and beginning their training for a marathon in the spring; they then use the summer to concentrate on shorter distances, and take part in track and field events.

If you are going to be a runner for the rest of your life, it is a good idea to vary your training like this during the year. This will keep you interested and motivated, and the variation is good for your overall fitness and health.

You should also aim to take one period of rest during the year. Ideally, cut back your running for around a month. During this time you might do some other sports such as swimming and cycling, or run occasionally but only for pleasure, without a stopwatch and definitely no speed work. This gives your body time to recover and rebuild itself. If you don't cut back for an easy period during the year, you may well find that your body does it for you, by imposing on you an injury or illness that stops you from running.

Conclusion

Running at different paces improves your fitness and running performance because it helps to increase the variety of ways in which your body adapts. It also increases the enjoyment you get out of the sport, by charting a galaxy of different ways you can train.

But the corollary of choice is complexity. We need to think carefully about how to combine these different training techniques to meet our goals. In this chapter we have navigated through the different considerations so that you can draw up your own training schedule that will help you to reach your goals in a way consistent with your personal circumstances. In the next chapter there are some sample training schedules, built up from these principles. You can use these as a basis for your own training schedules if you want, or you can build your own from scratch.

11 Racing

George Sheehan, the runner, writer and philosopher, said that the difference between a jogger and a runner is a race entry form.

Not everyone enjoys racing; but every runner should try it a few times. You don't need to be especially fast, or competitive.

Almost none of the runners in a race has any expectation of finishing first. Races are where we test ourselves, celebrate what we have achieved and face up to our own limitations. We engage in a personal struggle with ourselves, supported by the runners around us.

> 'The race is the tournament. It is the trial. The race for me is what the mountain is to the climber, what white water is to the canoeist. The race, where I can be a hero, is a contest where I give my word of honour to go out and do battle with myself'.
>
> *George Sheehan, Personal Best, 1989*

Choosing your first race

Your first task is to pick a suitable race. Obtain a copy of one of the running magazines (for example, *Runner's World*) that list races; or you can ask members of your local running club. Pick a race in your local area. Generally it is a good idea to start with a shorter distance such as 5 km. Women might consider the *Race for Life* women's 5 km race series, which raises money for cancer research. Avoid hilly courses for your first race. You will need to pick one that is sufficiently far in the future to give you plenty of time to train – aim for three to four months.

General racing tips

Running your first race can be pretty nerve-racking if you don't know what to expect. Here is the low-down.

- **Enter in advance**. Most races of half marathon or shorter can be entered on the day, but this can be a hassle. It is better to send off your entry form at least a week before the race, so that you get your race number through the post. Get the address of the organiser from *Runner's World*, or use a Universal Entry Form (which you will find in magazines or on the internet).

Packing list

- race clothes
- running shoes with orthotics
- running watch
- clean dry clothes, including t-shirt, underwear, socks
- change of shoes
- toilet roll

- Vaseline
- money
- bananas
- recovery drink
- safety pins
- race number
- bin liner to wear at start

- **Plan what to bring**. The night before the race, pin your number on your vest, and lay out your clothes on a chair. See the packing list.
- **Pin your number on the front of your shirt**. Cyclists pin their number on their back; runners on the front. This enables the organisers to record your finishing time.
- **Arrive early**. You don't want to feel rushed. Give yourself at least half an hour – preferably more – to change, go to the toilet, and hand in your bag.
- **Start slowly**. By far the most common mistake in races is to go shooting off with faster runners. Take it easy at first, and you can speed up towards the end if you still have the energy. According to Hal Higdon, one of the most prolific writers about marathons, every 10 seconds a mile you run too fast at the start of a marathon will cost you a minute a mile at the end.[51] When the starter's gun goes off, you will have to fight the temptation to be swept along in a rush of adrenaline. Maintain a comfortable pace, and chat with the runners around you. In the last mile or two, if you feel strong enough, you can really pick up your speed, and pass runners who have gone off too fast.
- **Don't weave**. If you find that the race is congested near the start, don't try to dodge through the runners. Wait for the field to spread out a bit, and then close down the gap later. Trying to overtake other runners at the start uses up energy, and encourages you to start too fast.

Helpers at a race

- **Finish looking good**. There will often be a photographer at the finish, and you want to look good in the photos of your first race. Look up and smile as you cross the finish line, and if you are switching off your stopwatch, don't obscure your running number.
- **Enjoy it**. Your first race is very special, and you will remember it for years to come.

'I once ran a ten mile race in a new pair of shoes. After 3 miles I got blisters. I spent the rest of the week hobbling around and couldn't run for a fortnight. So don't wear new shoes in races.'

Sally Hodge

Warming up and warming down

The purpose of **warming up** is to get your body prepared for running. The shorter the race, the more important it is to warm up.

Your metabolism takes some time to adjust to the higher level of energy output you need while you are racing. Your heart rate needs to increase, your blood distribution needs to be redirected to your muscles, and your temperature regulation system needs to adjust. If all this is happening in the early stages of the race, you will be performing below your full potential. If you start a race without warming up, your body will try to produce a lot of energy quickly and will have to use anaerobic metabolic pathways that produce lactic acid, which will cause you to fatigue quickly during the race.

Ideally, you should start to warm up about 30–40 minutes before the race. Jog a couple of miles, beginning very slowly and gradually increasing the speed to just below your threshold pace (see chapter 9). This will get your energy systems working. Then stretch quietly for 5–10 minutes, particularly the hamstrings, quads and calf muscles. Finally run up to a mile, at an easy pace but including some strides at your race pace. You should finish your warm-up about five minutes before the race is due to start. If the start is delayed, try to keep yourself moving, by running on the spot if necessary.

The exception to this is a race longer than the half marathon, for which you should do a much lighter warm-up. Because the limiting factor in these races is your energy stores, you don't want to start to deplete your glycogen before the race even starts. You may want to jog for half a mile, working up to your race pace, to get your metabolism going, but you should not do any high-intensity running before the race, as this uses mainly glycogen which you will need later on.

The purpose of '**warming down**' is to help your body return to normal after the race, and in particular to keep the blood flowing so that you clear the waste products from your system more quickly. After a short race, you should jog gently for 10–15 minutes at a very easy pace. If you are too tired to do this, you should try to walk briskly instead.

Again, the marathon is an exception. At the finish line of a marathon, few of us feel able to move at all, let alone jog. But as we shall see in the next chapter, you should at least try to keep moving after the finish, so that your muscles don't tighten up too much.

Predicting race times

It is a good idea to have some idea of how fast you can expect to finish a race, so that you know what pace to start at. If you are an experienced runner, you may be able to predict your race time from previous races, perhaps at different distances (either longer or shorter). There are various equations and tables based on evidence about how much runners slow down as the distance increases to help you do this. These are only guides, although they are sometimes remarkably accurate.

The following charts are based on comparing world record times. Any given race time is converted into a percentage of the world record pace for that distance – so the assumption is that if you are capable of running at 60 per cent of world record pace over 10 km, you can also run 60 per cent of world record pace over a half marathon. This assumption is clearly not valid unless you have trained for the distance you are racing.

The author

117

Table 11.1 Women's race time predictor chart

5 k	8 k	10 k	15 k	10 m	20 km	Half	Marathon
0:14:23	0:23:39	0:29:55	0:45:51	0:49:23	1:02:10	1:05:48	2:18:51
0:17:32	0:28:50	0:36:29	0:55:55	1:00;13	1·15·49	1:20:15	2:49.20
0:17:45	0:29:12	0:36:56	0:56:36	1:00:58	1:16:45	1:21:14	2:51:25
0:17:59	0:29:34	0:37:24	0:57:19	1:01:44	1:17:42	1:22:15	2:53:34
0:18:06	0:29:45	0:37:38	0:57:40	1:02:07	1:18:12	1:22:46	2:54:39
0:18:12	0:29:56	0:37:52	0:58:02	1:02:31	1:18:42	1:23:17	2:55:46
0:18:19	0:30:08	0:38:07	0:58:24	1:02:55	1:19:12	1:23:49	2:56:53
0:18:26	0:30:19	0:38:21	0:58:47	1:03:19	1:19:42	1:24:22	2:58:01
0:18:34	0:30:31	0:38:36	0:59:10	1:03:43	1:20:13	1:24:54	2:59:10
0:18:41	0:30:43	0:38:51	0:59:33	1:04:08	1:20:44	1:25:27	3:00:19
0:18:48	0:30:55	0:39:06	0:59:56	1:04:33	1:21:16	1:26:01	3:01:30
0:18:56	0:31:07	0:39:22	1:00:20	1:04:59	1:21:48	1:26:35	3:02:42
0:19:03	0:31:19	0:39:37	1:00:44	1:05:25	1:22:20	1:27:09	3:03:54
0:19:11	0:31:32	0:39:53	1:01:08	1:05:51	1:22:53	1:27:44	3:05:08
0:19:18	0:31:45	0:40:09	1:01:33	1:06:17	1:23:27	1:28:19	3:06:23
0:19:26	0:31:58	0:40:26	1:01:58	1:06:44	1:24:01	1:28:55	3:07:38
0:19:34	0:32:11	0:40:42	1:02:23	1:07:11	1:24:35	1:29:31	3:08:55
0:19:42	0:32:24	0:40:59	1:02:48	1:07:39	1:25:10	1:30:08	3:10:12
0:19:50	0:32:37	0:41:16	1:03:14	1:08:07	1:25:45	1:30:46	3:11:31
0:19:59	0:32:51	0:41:33	1:03:41	1:08:35	1:26:21	1:31:23	3:12:51
0:20:07	0:33:05	0:41:50	1:04:08	1:09:04	1:26:57	1:32:02	3:14:12
0:20:15	0:33:19	0:42:08	1:04:35	1:09:33	1:27:34	1:32:41	3:15:34
0:20:24	0:33:33	0:42:26	1:05:02	1:10:03	1:28:11	1:33:20	3:16:57
0:20:33	0:33:47	0:42:44	1:05:30	1:10:33	1:28:49	1:34:00	3:18:21
0:20:42	0:34:02	0:43:03	1:05:58	1:11:03	1:29:27	1:34:41	3:19:47
0:20:51	0:34:17	0:43:21	1:06:27	1:11:34	1:30:06	1:35:22	3:21:14
0:21:00	0:34:32	0:43:40	1:06:56	1:12:06	1:30:45	1:36:04	3:22:42
0:21:09	0:34:47	0:44:00	1:07:26	1:12:37	1:31:25	1:36:46	3:24:11
0:21:19	0:35:02	0:44:19	1:07:56	1:13:10	1:32:06	1:37:29	3:25:42
0:21:28	0:35:18	0:44:39	1:08:26	1:13:42	1:32:47	1:38:13	3:27:14
0:21:38	0:35:34	0:44:59	1:08:57	1:14:16	1:33:29	1:38:57	3:28:48
0:21:48	0:35:50	0:45:20	1:09:28	1:14:49	1:34:12	1:39:42	3:30:23
0:21:58	0:36:06	0:45:40	1:10:00	1:15:24	1:34:55	1:40:27	3:31:59
0:22:08	0:36:23	0:46:02	1:10:32	1:15:58	1:35:38	1:41:14	3:33:37
0:22:18	0:36:40	0:46:23	1:11:05	1:16:34	1:36:23	1:42:01	3:35:16
0:22:28	0:36:57	0:46:45	1:11:38	1:17:10	1:37:08	1:42:49	3:36:57
0:22:39	0:37:15	0:47:07	1:12:12	1:17:46	1:37:54	1:43:37	3:38:40
0:22:50	0:37:32	0:47:29	1:12:47	1:18:23	1:38:41	1:44:27	3:40:24
0:23:01	0:37:50	0:47:52	1:13:22	1:19:01	1:39:28	1:45:17	3:42:10
0:23:12	0:38:09	0:48:15	1:13:57	1:19:39	1:40:16	1:46:08	3:43:57

Table 11.1 Women's race time predictor chart – continued

5 k	8 k	10 k	15 k	10 m	20 km	Half	Marathon
0:23:23	0:38:27	0:48:39	1:14:33	1:20:18	1:41:05	1:47:00	3:45:46
0:23:35	0:38:46	0:49:03	1:15:10	1:20:57	1:41:55	1:47:52	3:47:37
0:23:46	0:39:05	0:49:27	1:15:47	1:21:38	1:42:45	1:48:46	3:49:30
0:23:58	0:39:25	0:49:52	1:16:25	1:22:18	1:43:37	1:49:40	3:51:25
0:24:10	0:39:45	0:50:17	1:17:04	1:23:00	1:44:29	1:50:35	3:53:22
0:24:23	0:40:05	0:50:42	1:17:43	1:23:42	1:45:22	1:51:32	3:55:20
0:24:35	0:40:26	0:51:08	1:18:23	1:24:25	1:46:16	1:52:29	3:57:21
0:24:48	0:40:47	0:51:35	1:19:03	1:25:09	1:47:11	1:53:27	3:59:24
0:25:01	0:41:08	0:52:02	1:19:44	1:25:53	1:48:07	1:54:26	4:01:29
0:25:14	0:41:29	0:52:29	1:20:26	1:26:38	1:49:04	1:55:26	4:03:36
0:25:27	0:41:52	0:52:57	1:21:09	1:27:24	1:50:02	1:56:28	4:05:45
0:25:41	0:42:14	0:53:25	1:21:52	1:28:11	1:51:01	1:57:30	4:07:57
0:25:55	0:42:37	0:53:54	1:22:37	1:28:59	1:52:01	1:58:34	4:10:11
0:26:09	0:43:00	0:54:24	1:23:22	1:29:47	1:53:02	1:59:38	4:12:27
0:26:23	0:43:24	0:54:54	1:24:08	1:30:37	1:54:04	2:00:44	4:14:46
0:26:38	0:43:48	0:55:24	1:24:54	1:31:27	1:55:07	2:01:51	4:17:08
0:26:53	0:44:12	0:55:55	1:25:42	1:32:18	1:56:12	2:02:59	4:19:32
0:27:08	0:44:37	0:56:27	1:26:31	1:33:11	1:57:18	2:04:09	4:21:59
0:27:24	0:45:03	0:56:59	1:27:20	1:34:04	1:58:25	2:05:20	4:24:29
0:27:40	0:45:29	0:57:32	1:28:10	1:34:58	1:59:33	2:06:32	4:27:01
0:27:56	0:45:55	0:58:05	1:29:02	1:35:53	2:00:43	2:07:46	4:29:37
0:28:12	0:46:22	0:58:40	1:29:54	1:36:50	2:01:54	2:09:01	4:32:15
0:28:29	0:46:50	0:59:14	1:30:48	1:37:47	2:03:06	2:10:18	4:34:57
0:28:46	0:47:18	0:59:50	1:31:42	1:38:46	2:04:20	2:11:36	4:37:42
0:29:03	0:47:47	1:00:26	1:32:38	1:39:46	2:05:35	2:12:56	4:40:30
0:29:21	0:48:16	1:01:03	1:33:34	1:40:47	2:06:52	2:14:17	4:43:22
0:29:39	0:48:46	1:01:41	1:34:32	1:41:49	2:08:11	2:15:40	4:46:17
0:29:58	0:49:16	1:02:20	1:35:31	1:42:53	2:09:31	2:17:05	4:49:16
0:30:17	0:49:47	1:02:59	1:36:32	1:43:58	2:10:53	2:18:32	4:52:19
0:30:36	0:50:19	1:03:39	1:37:33	1:45:04	2:12:16	2:20:00	4:55:26
0:30:56	0:50:52	1:04:20	1:38:36	1:46:12	2:13:42	2:21:30	4:58:36
0:31:16	0:51:25	1:05:02	1:39:40	1:47:21	2:15:09	2:23:03	5:01:51
0:31:37	0:51:59	1:05:45	1:40:46	1:48:32	2:16:38	2:24:37	5:05:10
0:31:58	0:52:33	1:06:29	1:41:53	1:49:44	2:18:09	2:26:13	5:08:33
0:32:19	0:53:09	1:07:14	1:43:02	1:50:58	2:19:42	2:27:52	5:12:01
0:32:41	0:53:45	1:08:00	1:44:12	1:52:14	2:21:17	2:29:33	5:15:34
0:33:04	0:54:22	1:08:46	1:45:24	1:53:31	2:22:55	2:31:16	5:19:12

Reproduced from Bob Glover and Shelly-lynn Florence Glover, *The Competitive Runner's Handbook*

Table 11.2 Men's race time predictor chart

5 k	8 k	10 k	15 k	10 m	20 km	Half	Marathon
0:12:58	0:21:19	0:26:58	0:41:26	0:44:40	0:56:20	0:59:03	2:06:50
0:15:49	0:26:00	0:32:53	0:50:32	0:54:28	1:08:42	1:12.01	2:34:40
0:16:00	0:26:19	0:33:18	0:51:09	0:55:09	1:09:33	1:12:54	2:36:35
0:16:12	0:26:39	0:33:42	0:51:47	0:55:50	1:10:25	1:13:49	2:38:32
0:16:19	0:26:49	0:33:55	0:52:07	0:56:11	1:10:52	1:14:17	2:39:32
0:16:25	0:26:59	0:34:08	0:52:27	0:56:32	1:11:18	1:14:45	2:40:33
0:16:31	0:27:09	0:34:21	0:52:47	0:56:54	1:11:46	1:15:13	2:41:34
0:16:37	0:27:20	0:34:34	0:53:07	0:57:16	1:12:13	1:15:42	2:42:36
0:16:44	0:27:30	0:34:48	0:53:28	0:57:38	1:12:41	1:16:12	2:43:39
0:16:50	0:27:41	0:35:01	0:53:49	0:58:01	1:13:10	1:16:41	2:44:43
0:16:57	0:27:52	0:35:15	0:54:10	0:58:23	1:13:38	1:17:11	2:45:48
0:17:04	0:28:03	0:35:29	0:54:31	0:58:46	1:14:07	1:17:42	2:46:53
0:17:10	0:28:14	0:35:43	0:54:53	0:59:10	1:14:37	1:18:13	2:47:59
0:17:17	0:28:25	0:35:57	0:55:15	0:59:33	1:15:07	1:18:44	2:49:07
0:17:24	0:28:37	0:36:12	0:55:37	0:59:57	1:15:37	1:19:16	2:50:15
0:17:31	0:28:48	0:36:26	0:55:59	1:00:22	1:16:08	1:19:48	2:51:24
0:17:39	0:29:00	0:36:41	0:56:22	1:00:46	1:16:39	1:20:20	2:52:34
0:17:46	0:29:12	0:36:56	0:56:45	1:01:11	1:17:10	1:20:53	2:53:45
0:17:53	0:29:24	0:37:12	0:57:09	1:01:37	1:17:42	1:21:27	2:54:57
0:18:01	0:29:36	0:37:27	0:57:33	1:02:02	1:18:14	1:22:01	2:56:09
0:18:08	0:29:49	0:37:43	0:57:57	1:02:28	1:18:47	1:22:35	2:57:23
0:18:16	0:30:01	0:37:59	0:58:21	1:02:55	1:19:21	1:23:10	2:58:38
0:18:24	0:30:14	0:38:15	0:58:46	1:03:21	1:19:54	1:23:46	2:59:54
0:18:31	0:30:27	0:38:31	0:59:11	1:03:49	1:20:29	1:24:21	3:01:11
0:18:39	0:30:40	0:38:48	0:59:37	1:04:16	1:21:03	1:24:58	3:02:30
0:18:48	0:30:54	0:39:05	1:00:03	1:04:44	1:21:39	1:25:35	3:03:49
0:18:56	0:31:07	0:39:22	1:00:29	1:05:12	1:22:14	1:26:12	3:05:09
0:19:04	0:31:21	0:39:39	1:00:56	1:05:41	1:22:51	1:26:50	3:06:31
0:19:13	0:31:35	0:39:57	1:01:23	1:06:10	1:23:27	1:27:29	3:07:54
0:19:21	0:31:49	0:40:15	1:01:50	1:06:40	1:24:05	1:28:08	3:09:18
0:19:30	0:32:03	0:40:33	1:02:18	1:07:10	1:24:43	1:28:48	3:10:44
0:19:39	0:32:18	0:40:52	1:02:47	1:07:41	1:25:21	1:29:28	3:12:10
0:19:48	0:32:33	0:41:10	1:03:15	1:08:12	1:26:00	1:30:09	3:13:38
0:19:57	0:32:48	0:41:29	1:03:45	1:08:43	1:26:40	1:30:51	3:15:08
0:20:06	0:33:03	0:41:49	1:04:14	1:09:15	1:27:20	1:31:33	3:16:38
0:20:16	0:33:18	0:42:08	1:04:44	1:09:48	1:28:01	1:32:16	3:18:11
0:20:25	0:33:34	0:42:28	1:05:15	1:10:20	1:28:43	1:33:00	3:19:44
0:20:35	0:33:50	0:42:48	1:05:46	1:10:54	1:29:25	1:33:44	3:21:19
0:20:45	0:34:06	0:43:09	1:06:18	1:11:28	1:30:08	1:34:29	3:22:56
0:20:55	0:34:23	0:43:30	1:06:50	1:12:03	1:30:52	1:35:15	3:24:34

Table 11.2 Men's race time predictor chart – continued

5 k	8 k	10 k	15 k	10 m	20 km	Half	Marathon
0:21:05	0:34:40	0:43:51	1:07:22	1:12:38	1:31:36	1:36:01	3:26:14
0:21:15	0:34:57	0:44:12	1:07:55	1:13:13	1:32:21	1:36:48	3:27:55
0:21:26	0:35:14	0:44:34	1:08:29	1:13:50	1:33:07	1:37:36	3:29:39
0:21:37	0:35:32	0:44:57	1:09:03	1:14:27	1:33:53	1:38:25	3:31:23
0:21:48	0:35:50	0:45:19	1:09:38	1:15:04	1:34:41	1:39:15	3:33:10
0:21:59	0:36:08	0:45:42	1:10:14	1:15:42	1:35:29	1:40:05	3:34:58
0:22:10	0:36:26	0:46:06	1:10:50	1:16:21	1:36:18	1:40:56	3:36:49
0:22:21	0:36:45	0:46:30	1:11:26	1:17:01	1:37:08	1:41:49	3:38:41
0:22:33	0:37:04	0:46:54	1:12:03	1:17:41	1:37:58	1:42:42	3:40:35
0:22:45	0:37:24	0:47:19	1:12:41	1:18:22	1:38:50	1:43:36	3:42:31
0:22:57	0:37:44	0:47:44	1:13:20	1:19:03	1:39:42	1:44:31	3:44:29
0:23:09	0:38:04	0:48:09	1:13:59	1:19:46	1:40:36	1:45:27	3:46:29
0:23:22	0:38:25	0:48:35	1:14:39	1:20:29	1:41:30	1:46:24	3:48:32
0:23:35	0:38:45	0:49:02	1:15:20	1:21:13	1:42:25	1:47:22	3:50:36
0:23:48	0:39:07	0:49:29	1:16:01	1:21:57	1:43:22	1:48:21	3:52:43
0:24:01	0:39:29	0:49:56	1:16:44	1:22:43	1:44:19	1:49:21	3:54:53
0:24:14	0:39:51	0:50:24	1:17:27	1:23:29	1:45:18	1:50:22	3:57:04
0:24:28	0:40:13	0:50:53	1:18:11	1:24:17	1:46:17	1:51:25	3:59:18
0:24:42	0:40:36	0:51:22	1:18:55	1:25:05	1:47:18	1:52:29	4:01:35
0:24:56	0:41:00	0:51:52	1:19:41	1:25:54	1:48:20	1:53:33	4:03:55
0:25:11	0:41:23	0:52:22	1:20:27	1:26:44	1:49:23	1:54:40	4:06:17
0:25:25	0:41:48	0:52:53	1:21:15	1:27:35	1:50:27	1:55:47	4:08:42
0:25:41	0:42:13	0:53:24	1:22:03	1:28:27	1:51:33	1:56:56	4:11:09
0:25:56	0:42:38	0:53:56	1:22:52	1:29:20	1:52:40	1:58:06	4:13:40
0:26:12	0:43:04	0:54:29	1:23:42	1:30:14	1:53:48	1:59:18	4:16:14
0:26:28	0:43:30	0:55:02	1:24:33	1:31:09	1:54:58	2:00:31	4:18:51
0:26:44	0:43:57	0:55:36	1:25:26	1:32:06	1:56:09	2:01:45	4:21:31
0:27:01	0:44:25	0:56:11	1:26:19	1:33:03	1:57:22	2:03:01	4:24:14
0:27:18	0:44:53	0:56:46	1:27:14	1:34:02	1:58:36	2:04:19	4:27:01
0:27:35	0:45:21	0:57:23	1:28:09	1:35:02	1:59:51	2:05:38	4:29:51
0:27:53	0:45:51	0:58:00	1:29:06	1:36:03	2:01:09	2:06:59	4:32:46
0:28:11	0:46:20	0:58:37	1:30:04	1:37:06	2:02:28	2:08:22	4:35:43
0:28:30	0:46:51	0:59:16	1:31:04	1:38:10	2:03:49	2:09:47	4:38:45
0:28:49	0:47:22	0:59:56	1:32:04	1:39:16	2:05:11	2:11:13	4:41:51
0:29:08	0:47:54	1:00:36	1:33:07	1:40:22	2:06:36	2:12:42	4:45:01
0:29:28	0:48:27	1:01:17	1:34:10	1:41:31	2:08:02	2:14:12	4:48:15
0:29:49	0:49:00	1:02:00	1:35:15	1:42:41	2:09:30	2:15:45	4:51:34

Reproduced from Bob Glover and Shelly-lynn Florence Glover, *The Competitive Runner's Handbook*

Racing 5km

The 5 km is now a popular distance – partly because of the success in the UK of the *Race for Life* series of women-only races, which raise money for cancer research. In London, there is a well-attended lunchtime 5 km in Hyde Park on the last Friday of every month.

Races over this distance can be intense; but they don't stress the body as much as longer races, enabling you to continue training, or race again the next week if you want to. They are suitable for beginners because they don't require an enormous level of fitness; but they are also an excellent test for more experienced runners.

Training for a 5 km race

Although the distance is relatively short, you still need a good base of endurance running and strength for a 5 km training programme, so that you can do the speed training safely and well.

Your programme should begin with a month of base aerobic training, then strength training, before you start the speed work.

When you get to the speed work, do plenty of short, fast intervals. While beginners should not do more than one speed session a week, for more experienced runners it is helpful to include a second speed session during the week if possible.

The sample training programmes on the following pages will help you to put together a schedule.

5 km races

You need to warm up thoroughly for a 5 km race – run at least a mile at moderate pace. Dress in cool clothes, because you will get hot quickly in fast races. It is not necessary to eat or drink in a 5 km race.

Racing 10 km

The 10 km is one of the classic running distances; there are plenty of races at this distance to choose from, and because recovery is quick you can run a 10 km every weekend. The 10 km is an interesting combination of speed and endurance.

Training for a 10 km

Training for a 10 km involves more mileage, and less speed work, than training for a 5 km. To race at this distance you need to be running between 20 and 60 miles a week; and you need a long run of at least 7 miles, and preferably more like 12 miles, at least once a fortnight.

It is a good idea to do some races in the build-up to your 10 km race – perhaps a 5 km for speed, and a longer race (e.g. a half marathon) for endurance. Any race you do during the build-up to a 10 km should not be longer than a half marathon, as this will do you more harm than good.

Racing the 10 km

You should warm up well before a 10 km. Make sure you drink plenty of water the night before, and up to two hours before the race. Faster runners will not drink at all during a 10 km. Most mid-pack runners should reckon to sip some water once or twice during the race, but you don't need to drink a lot on a race of this duration.

The key to running a good 10 km is running the first mile at the right speed. Too fast and you will throw away your chance of finishing strong in the final miles. Too slow, and you will struggle to make up the lost time in the closing stages. My view is that you should run the first mile a few seconds a mile slower than the overall speed you need for your target time.

Many runners sag in the middle stages of the 10 km. At this point you begin to tire; but you are not close enough to the finish to allow yourself to go full out. Concentrate on your form and your breathing, and maintaining a steady pace.

Racing half marathons

This is my favourite distance. The UK's largest mass participation road race is a half marathon (the Great North Run, from Newcastle to South Shields), which reflects the popularity of the distance. It is sufficiently far to be a serious challenge, even to experienced runners. But you can recover from a half marathon in a fortnight, unlike the marathon, from which it can take several months to recover fully.

The half marathon pace is very close to your aerobic threshold (see chapter 10), which means that running at this pace enhances your overall aerobic performance, and so improves your fitness and running at all distances. The half marathon is also an essential stepping-stone for anyone interested in running a full marathon. It builds confidence and racing experience, and helps you to judge what you will be able to achieve in a longer race.

Training for the half marathon

If you want to train seriously for a half marathon you will need to do at least 16 weeks of training, beginning with at least a month of aerobic running. Beginners should be running 30 miles a week, and serious runners nearly 70 miles a week. Runners of all standards need to include a long run at least three times a month, of between 10 and 18 miles.

Speed training for a half marathon inevitably involves slower, longer repetitions than for the 10 km, with efforts between 800 m and 3 km. It is a good idea to race a 10 km in the build-up to your half marathon, to test your endurance and sharpen your speed.

You should reduce your running considerably in the last two weeks before a half marathon race. This tapering will help you to build muscle glycogen and rehydrate, and ensure that your legs are fresh for the race.

Racing the half marathon

Because this is a long race, you don't need to warm up much before the start. Your task is to preserve your stored energy. You may want to jog for half a mile before the race to loosen up your muscles and get your metabolism going, but you should not do any intense running before the start.

All runners should drink water during a half marathon. The general guidelines on drinking during races apply: drink little and often, right from the gun. Don't wait until you feel thirsty to start drinking.

The half marathon is long enough to give you plenty of time to catch up if you start slowly. The pace of a half marathon will generally seem slow at first, because you

> 'Don't worry about the miles you have that are behind you: only think about the miles you have still to go. Keep focused on what is ahead. That is the best way to get your pacing right.'
>
> *Nick Slade, ultramarathoner*

are used to running faster for short runs. But if you go off too fast, you will pay the price in the closing stages of the run. You are racing at your aerobic threshold – if you push too fast you will kick into anaerobic metabolism and lactate build-up, and once you have 'blown' you will find it very difficult to regain your equilibrium.

So go out slowly, and ease into the race. Try to get in step with some other runners who are going at about your pace. Let runners go past you for the first few miles: you will probably overtake them in the last few miles. After the second or third mile (not before) you should reach your target pace, which you can hold for most of the race. Try to avoid sagging during miles 6–9. Don't just keep pace with the runners around you, because they might well be slowing down during the second half, just when you should be speeding up.

At the ten-mile mark, you have only the equivalent of a 5 km to complete. Begin to increase your pace, identify runners ahead of you and begin to close them down. Don't accelerate too much – try to remain on the right side of your threshold. In the final mile, push hard, and remember all the speed work you have done on the track.

Conclusion

Racing is definitely pretty scary for anyone who hasn't tried it. Most of us don't want to be competitive in our running, so why should we race?

Once you've tried it, however, racing is highly addictive. In part it is the pleasure of a measured course, with signposts and marshals and water tables. In part it is the fun of making new friends, and meeting up with old friends, and running with a large group of people. But most of all, racing helps us to see how we are progressing, to do battle with our bodies and our minds, under the unbiased eye of the stopwatch.

I was a jogger for many years. One day, a colleague persuaded me to take part in a 10 km race. Because we were living in Africa, and it was too hot to run during the day, this race took place at 6 o'clock on a Sunday morning. I cursed him as I struggled out of bed at 4.30am to have something to eat, and found my way in the dark to the start. The race began just as the sun rose over the horizon. It took me 50 minutes to run that 10 km, and it was one of the most exhilarating experiences of my life. By 7 o'clock that morning, I was hooked, chatting excitedly with my new friends about which races we could do the next weekend. I had become a runner.

Training schedules for 5 km, 10 km and half marathon

Table 11.3 Sample training schedule for 5 km: beginner

Weeks	Phase	Miles	Mon	Tue	Wed	Thu	Fri	Sat	Sun
Base	Base	13		3 easy	3 thresh			3 easy	4 slow
12	Base	15		4 easy	4 thresh			3 easy	4 slow
11	Strength	16		3 hills	3 easy	3 thresh		3 easy	4 slow
10	Strength	18		3 hills	4 easy	3 fartlek		4 easy	4 slow
9	Strength	19		4 hills	4 easy	3 thresh		2 easy	6 race
8	Strength E	15		3 hills	3 easy	3 fartlek		3 easy	3 slow
7	Speed	18		3 thresh	4 easy	3 interval		3 easy	5 slow
6	Speed	20		4 fartlek	4 easy	4 interval		4 easy	4 slow
5	Speed	20		3 thresh	4 easy	4 interval		4 easy	5 slow
4	Speed E	14		3 fartlek	4 easy	2 interval		2 easy	3 slow
3	Peak	17		3 fartlek	4 easy	4 interval		2 easy	4 slow
2	Peak	11		3 fartlek	3 easy	1 interval			4 slow
1	Race	11		3 strides	3 easy	2 easy			3 race

Sample interval sessions:

Wk 7   3 sets of 4 × 400 m at 800 m pace; 150 sec recovery; 1 lap jog between sets

Wk 6   2 sets of 3 × 1000 m at 3 km pace; 120 sec recovery; 1 lap jog between sets

Wk 5   400 m, 600 m, 800 m, 1200 m, 1600 m, 1200 m, 800 m, 600 m, 400 m (+5 sec/lap as +distance); 60 sec recovery

Wk 4   6 × 600 m at 1500 m pace; 120 sec recovery

Wk 3   4 × 1600 m at 5 km pace; 90 sec recovery

Wk 2   10 × 200 m at 400 m pace; 180 sec recovery

Table 11.4 Sample training schedule for 5 km: intermediate

Weeks	Phase	Miles	Mon	Tue	Wed	Thu	Fri	Sat	Sun
Base	Base	16		4 easy	3 thresh			4 easy	5 slow
12	Base E	14		4 easy	3 thresh			3 easy	4 slow
11	Strength	18		3 hills	4 easy	3 thresh		3 easy	5 slow
10	Strength	20		3 hills	4 easy	3 fartlek		4 easy	6 slow
9	Strength	22		4 hills	5 easy	3 thresh		4 easy	6 race
8	Strength E	16		2 hills	3 easy	3 fartlek		3 easy	5 slow
7	Speed	23		4 thresh	4 easy	3 interval		4 easy	8 slow
6	Speed	25		5 fartlek	4 easy	4 interval		5 easy	7 slow
5	Speed	25		4 thresh	4 easy	4 interval		5 easy	8 slow
4	Speed E	16		3 fartlek	4 easy	2 interval		2 easy	5 slow
3	Peak	23		3 fartlek	4 easy	4 interval		4 easy	8 slow
2	Peak	17		3 fartlek	4 easy	1 interval		4 easy	5 slow
1	Race	14		3 strides	4 easy	4 easy			3 race

Sample interval sessions:
Wk 7   3 sets of 4 × 400 m at 800 m pace; 150 sec recovery; 1 lap jog between sets
Wk 6   2 sets of 3 × 1000 m at 3 km pace; 120 sec recovery; 1 lap jog between sets
Wk 5   400 m, 600 m, 800 m, 1200 m, 1600 m, 1200 m, 800 m, 600 m, 400 m (+5 sec/lap as +distance); 60 sec recovery
Wk 4   6 × 600 m at 1500 m pace; 120 sec recovery
Wk 3   4 × 1600 m at 5 km pace; 90 sec recovery
Wk 2   10 × 200 m at 400 m pace; 180 sec recovery

Table 11.5 Sample training schedule for 5 km: advanced

Weeks	Phase	Miles	Mon	Tue	Wed	Thu	Fri	Sat	Sun
Base	Base	25		5 easy	3 thresh	4 easy		4 easy	9 slow
12	Base E	20	3 easy	4 easy	3thresh	3 easy		3 easy	4 slow
11	Strength	27	4 easy	3 hills	4 easy	4 thresh		3 easy	9 slow
10	Strength	29	4 easy	3 hills	4 easy	4 fartlek		4 easy	10 slow
9	Strength	28	5 easy	4 hills	5 easy	4 thresh		4 easy	6 race
8	Strength E	20	4 easy	2 hills	3 easy	3 fartlek		3 easy	5 slow
7	Speed	31	5 easy	4 thresh	5 easy	3 interval		4 easy	10 slow
6	Speed	35	5 easy	5 fartlek	4 easy	4 interval		5 easy	12 slow
5	Speed	33	5 easy	4 thresh	5 easy	4 interval		5 easy	10 slow
4	Speed E	20	4 easy	3 fartlek	4 easy	2 interval		2 easy	5 slow
3	Peak	33	5 easy	3 fartlek	5 easy	4 interval		4 easy	12 slow
2	Peak	26	5 easy	3 fartlek	5 easy	1 interval		4 easy	8 slow
1	Race	18	4 easy	3 strides	4 easy	4 easy			3 race

Sample interval sessions:

Wk 7 3 sets of 4 × 400 m at 800 m pace; 150 sec recovery; 1 lap jog between sets

Wk 6 2 sets of 3 × 1000 m at 3 km pace; 120 sec recovery; 1 lap jog between sets

Wk 5 400 m, 600 m, 800 m, 1200 m, 1600 m, 800 m, 600 m, 400 m (+5 sec/lap as +distance); 60 sec recovery

Wk 4 6 × 600 m at 1500 m pace; 120 sec recovery

Wk 3 4 × 1600 m at 5 km pace; 90 sec recovery

Wk 2 10 × 200 m at 400 m pace; 180 sec recovery

Table 11.6 Sample training schedule for 10 km: beginner

Weeks	Phase	Miles	Mon	Tue	Wed	Thu	Fri	Sat	Sun
Base	Base	16		4 easy	3 thresh			3 easy	6 slow
12	Base E	12		3 easy	3 fartlek			3 easy	3 slow
11	Strength	17		2 hills	3 easy	3 thresh		3 easy	6 slow
10	Strength	18		3 hills	4 easy	3 fartlek		3 easy	5 slow
9	Strength	20		3 hills	4 easy	4 thresh		3 easy	6 race
8	Strength E	14		2 hills	3 easy	4 fartlek			5 slow
7	Speed	21		3 thresh	4 easy	3 interval		3 easy	8 slow
6	Speed	20		4 fartlek	4 easy	4 interval		3 easy	5 slow
5	Speed	21		3 thresh	4 easy	3 interval		4 easy	7 slow
4	Speed E	16		3 fartlek	4 easy	2 interval		3 easy	4 slow
3	Peak	21		3 fartlek	4 easy	4 interval		3 easy	7 slow
2	Peak	16		3 fartlek	4 easy	1 interval		3 easy	5 slow
1	Race	14		3 strides	3 easy	2 easy			6 race

Sample interval sessions:

Wk 7   3 sets of 4 × 400 m at 800 m pace; 150 sec recovery; 1 lap jog between sets

Wk 6   2 sets of 3 × 1000 m at 3 km pace; 120 sec recovery; 1 lap jog between sets

Wk 5   400 m, 600 m, 800 m, 1200 m, 1600 m, 1200 m, 800 m, 600 m, 400 m (+5 sec/lap as +distance); 60 sec recovery

Wk 4   6 × 600 m at 1500 m pace; 120 sec recovery

Wk 3   4 × 1600 m at 5 km pace; 90 sec recovery

Wk 2   10 × 200 m at 400 m pace; 180 sec recovery

Table 11.7 Sample training schedule for 10 km: intermediate

Weeks	Phase	Miles	Mon	Tue	Wed	Thu	Fri	Sat	Sun
Base	Base	21		5 easy	3 thresh			5 easy	8 slow
12	Base E	17		4 easy	3 thresh			4 easy	6 slow
11	Strength	22		3 hills	5 easy	3 thresh		5 easy	6 slow
10	Strength	24		3 hills	5 easy	3 fartlek		5 easy	8 slow
9	Strength	26		4 hills	5 easy	4 thresh			13 race
8	Strength E	18		2 hills	3 easy	3 fartlek		3 easy	7 slow
7	Speed	26		4 thresh	4 easy	3 interval		5 easy	10 slow
6	Speed	28		5 fartlek	5 easy	4 interval		6 easy	8 slow
5	Speed	29		4 thresh	5 easy	4 interval		6 easy	10 slow
4	Speed E	22		4 fartlek	4 easy	2 interval		4 easy	8 slow
3	Peak	30		4 fartlek	6 easy	4 interval		6 easy	10 slow
2	Peak	19		4 fartlek	4 easy	1 interval		4 easy	6 slow
1	Race	16		3 strides	4 easy	3 easy			6 race

Sample interval sessions:

Wk 7   3 sets of 4 × 400 m at 800 m pace; 150 sec recovery; 1 lap jog between sets
Wk 6   2 sets of 3 × 1000 m at 3 km pace; 120 sec recovery; 1 lap jog between sets
Wk 5   400 m, 600 m, 800 m, 1200 m, 1600 m, 1200 m, 800 m, 600 m, 400 m (+5 sec/lap as +distance); 60 sec recovery
Wk 4   6 × 600 m at 1500 m pace; 120 sec recovery
Wk 3   4 × 1600 m at 5 km pace; 90 sec recovery
Wk 2   10 × 200 m at 400 m pace; 180 sec recovery

Table 11.8 Sample training schedule for 10 km: advanced

Weeks	Phase	Miles	Mon	Tue	Wed	Thu	Fri	Sat	Sun
Base	Base	30		6 easy	4 thresh	5 easy		5 easy	10 slow
12	Base E	22	3 easy	4 easy	3 thresh	3 easy		3 easy	6 slow
11	Strength	32	5 easy	3 hills	5 easy	4 thresh		5 easy	10 slow
10	Strength	33	5 easy	3 hills	5 easy	4 fartlek		5 easy	11 slow
9	Strength	35	6 easy	4 hills	5 easy	4 thresh		3 easy	13 race
8	Strength E	27	5 easy	2 hills	5 easy	3 fartlek		4 easy	8 slow
7	Speed	37	6 easy	4 thresh	7 easy	3 interval		5 easy	12 slow
6	Speed	40	6 easy	5 fartlek	6 easy	4 interval		5 easy	14 slow
5	Speed	39	6 easy	4 thresh	6 easy	4 interval		5 easy	14 slow
4	Speed E	28	6 easy	3 fartlek	5 easy	2 interval		4 easy	8 slow
3	Peak	40	7 easy	3 fartlek	7 easy	4 interval		5 easy	14 slow
2	Peak	28	6 easy	3 fartlek	6 easy	1 interval		4 easy	8 slow
1	Race	21	4 easy	3 strides	4 easy	4 easy			6 race

Sample interval sessions:
Wk 7 3 sets of 4 × 400 m at 800 m pace; 150 sec recovery; 1 lap jog between sets
Wk 6 2 sets of 3 × 1000 m at 3 km pace; 120 sec recovery; 1 lap jog between sets
Wk 5 400 m, 600 m, 800 m, 1200 m, 1600 m, 1200 m, 800 m, 600 m, 400 m (+5 sec/lap as +distance); 60 sec recovery
Wk 4 6 × 600 m at 1500 m pace; 120 sec recovery
Wk 3 4 × 1600 m at 5 km pace; 90 sec recovery
Wk 2 10 × 200 m at 400 m pace; 180 sec recovery

Table 11.9 Sample training schedule for half marathon: beginner

Weeks	Phase	Miles	Mon	Tue	Wed	Thu	Fri	Sat	Sun
Base	Base	20		5 easy	3 thresh			4 easy	8 slow
12	Base E	15		4 easy	3 fartlek			3 easy	5 slow
11	Strength	20		2 hills	4 easy	3 thresh		5 easy	6 slow
10	Strength	22		3 hills	4 easy	3 fartlek		4 easy	8 slow
9	Strength	24		3 hills	4 easy	3 thresh		1 stride	13 race
8	Strength E	16		2 hills	2 easy	4 fartlek		2 easy	6 slow
7	Speed	25		3 thresh	4 easy	3 interval		3 easy	12 slow
6	Speed	23		4 fartlek	4 easy	4 interval		3 easy	8 slow
5	Speed	25		3 thresh	4 easy	3 interval		3 easy	12 slow
4	Speed E	18		3 fartlek	4 easy	2 interval		3 easy	6 slow
3	Peak	26		3 fartlek	4 easy	4 interval		3 easy	12 slow
2	Peak	20		4 fartlek	4 easy	1 interval		3 easy	8 slow
1	Race	20		3 strides	2 easy	2 easy			13 race

Sample interval sessions:

Wk 7 3 sets of 4 × 400 m at 800 m pace; 150 sec recovery; 1 lap jog between sets

Wk 6 2 sets of 3 × 1000 m at 3 km pace; 120 sec recovery; 1 lap jog between sets

Wk 5 400 m, 600 m, 800 m, 1200 m, 1600 m, 1200 m, 800 m, 600 m, 400 m (+5 sec/lap as +distance); 60 sec recovery

Wk 4 6 × 600 m at 1500 m pace; 120 sec recovery

Wk 3 4 × 1600 m at 5 km pace; 90 sec recovery

Wk 2 10 × 200 m at 400 m pace; 180 sec recovery

Table 11.10 Sample training schedule for half marathon: intermediate

Weeks	Phase	Miles	Mon	Tue	Wed	Thu	Fri	Sat	Sun
Base	Base	24		6 easy	4 thresh			6 easy	8 slow
12	Base E	18		5 easy	3 thresh			4 easy	6 slow
11	Strength	24		3 hills	5 easy	3 thresh		5 easy	8 slow
10	Strength	26		3 hills	5 easy	3 fartlek		5 easy	10 slow
9	Strength	29		4 hills	5 easy	3 thresh		4 easy	13 race
8	Strength E	21		4 hills	3 easy	3 fartlek		3 easy	8 slow
7	Speed	31		4 thresh	4 easy	3 interval		6 easy	14 slow
6	Speed	30		5 fartlek	5 easy	4 interval		6 easy	10 slow
5	Speed	33		4 thresh	5 easy	4 interval		6 easy	14 slow
4	Speed E	24		4 fartlek	4 easy	2 interval		6 easy	8 slow
3	Peak	32		4 fartlek	4 easy	4 interval		6 easy	14 slow
2	Taper	21		4 fartlek	4 easy	1 interval		6 easy	6 slow
1	Race	24		3 strides	4 easy	4 easy			13 race

Sample interval sessions:

Wk 7   3 sets of 4 × 400 m at 800 m pace; 150 sec recovery; 1 lap jog between sets

Wk 6   2 sets of 3 × 1000 m at 3 km pace; 120 sec recovery; 1 lap jog between sets

Wk 5   400 m, 600 m, 800 m, 1200 m, 1600 m, 1200 m, 800 m, 600 m, 400 m (+5 sec/lap as +distance); 60 sec recovery

Wk 4   6 × 600 m at 1500 m pace; 120 sec recovery

Wk 3   4 × 1600 m at 5 km pace; 90 sec recovery

Wk 2   10 × 200 m at 400 m pace; 180 sec recovery

Table 11.11 Sample training schedule for half marathon: advanced

Weeks	Phase	Miles	Mon	Tue	Wed	Thu	Fri	Sat	Sun
Base	Base	34		6 easy	4 thresh	6 easy		6 easy	12 slow
12	Base E	26	3 easy	4 easy	3 thresh	4 easy		4 easy	8 slow
11	Strength	34	5 easy	3 hills	5 easy	4 thresh		5 easy	12 slow
10	Strength	35	6 easy	3 hills	5 easy	4 fartlek		5 easy	12 slow
9	Strength	37	6 easy	4 hills	5 easy	4 thresh		5 easy	13 race
8	Strength E	28	6 easy	2 hills	5 easy	3 fartlek		5 easy	7 slow
7	Speed	39	6 easy	4 thresh	7 easy	3 interval		5 easy	14 slow
6	Speed	42	6 easy	5 fartlek	6 easy	4 interval		5 easy	16 slow
5	Speed	44	6 easy	4 thresh	7 easy	4 interval		5 easy	18 slow
4	Speed E	28	4 easy	3 fartlek	4 easy	2 interval		5 easy	10 slow
3	Peak	44	7 easy	3 fartlek	7 easy	4 interval		5 easy	18 slow
2	Taper	25	5 easy	3 fartlek	6 easy	1 interval		3 easy	7 slow
1	Race	21	4 easy	3 strides	4 easy	4 easy			6 race

Sample interval sessions:

Wk 7 3 sets of 4 × 400 m at 800 m pace; 150 sec recovery; 1 lap jog between sets

Wk 6 2 sets of 3 × 1000 m at 3 km pace; 120 sec recovery; 1 lap jog between sets

Wk 5 400 m, 600 m, 800 m, 1200 m, 1600 m, 1200 m, 800 m, 600 m, 400 m (+5 sec/lap as +distance); 60 sec recovery

Wk 4 6 × 600 m at 1500 m pace; 120 sec recovery

Wk 3 4 × 1600 m at 5 km pace; 90 sec recovery

Wk 2 10 × 200 m at 400 m pace; 180 sec recovery

Running a marathon is one of the most challenging and rewarding events that any of us will experience. The human body imposes natural limitations on the distance we can run easily. Twenty miles is about the furthest we can go comfortably, even if we are well trained, before we begin to run out of fuel and our muscles begin to hurt. The marathon distance is exquisitely set to take us beyond our comfort zone, into a realm in which we confront the limitations of our bodies and our minds. We complete the marathon distance only by patient preparation and mental discipline. There are no short cuts, no easy ways out. The marathon takes us up to, and beyond, the limit of human endurance, into an unknown zone where we confront our true selves, and discover our inner strengths and limits.

Why run a marathon?

Thirty-five thousand people run the London Marathon each year, and tens of thousands of runners also take part in big city marathons such as New York, Paris, Boston and Sydney. Why do we all do it? There is something about the challenge of the marathon that attracts our sense of adventure.

Most participants in a marathon just want to finish. They may run the whole distance; more likely they will run and walk, just as long as they get round. These are the real heroes of the marathon – the runners who have risen to a challenge unlike anything they have done before. They may be running for charity, perhaps in memory of a loved one, or to show themselves and the world that they have the inner strength to succeed.

The next group of marathon runners want to perform and improve. These are often club runners, and they may well have run a marathon before, and now want to finish in a faster time (or at least fight off the effects of advancing age by finishing no slower). The pressure is enormous: they train for months, focused on a single race. If they happen to have a bad day, it will be another six months before they have their next chance to achieve their goals and recover their pride and confidence.

The third and final group of runners are the elite racers, hoping to do well, or perhaps win, at least in their age group. Again, their opportunities to achieve their goals are rare. Unless they are blessed with an extraordinary physiology, marathon athletes may have as few as eight or ten good marathon races in their whole lifetime; some have as few as two or three.

There are plenty of good reasons for training for and running a marathon. The training will help you to lose weight and increase your fitness. Running will bring you more self-confidence and energy. Achieving such a demanding goal will earn you self-respect, and the esteem of others around you.

One of the excitements and pleasures of the marathon is that all these runners take part in the same race, with the same sense of occasion. All know that, in different ways, they are facing up to their own challenge.

Which football-lover has played in a team with his or her football idol? Which hockey player has skated with the great names of hockey? As a runner, I've been privileged to take part in races with my heroes, including Paula Radcliffe, Josiah Tugwane, Bill Rodgers and Haile Gebreselassie. They beat me, for sure, but we were all part of it together.

Training for the marathon

Most people who are not very unfit can run a 5 km or a 10 km without too much difficulty. They might not do it very fast, and they might not enjoy it much, but they will get themselves round. The marathon is different. You don't need to be a great athlete to run a marathon. But you do need to train properly and sensibly. If you take the time to train, you will finish and achieve your goal.

You can put together your own marathon training programme using the guidance in chapters 9 and 10. Because the marathon is unique, and so popular, there are also several books devoted to training for it. Hal Higdon's *Marathon* is one of the best-known, and is excellent.

Before you start training

- Ideally, you should be running at least three times a week for at least a year, preferably two, before you start training for a marathon; you should be able to run 10 miles comfortably before you start a marathon training programme;
- think it through carefully and discuss it with your family; training for a marathon is a considerable commitment – make sure you have the support of those around you; plan reward days, and days off, which you will spend with your partner or family, and build these into your training plan;
- check the list on page 8 to see if you should consult your doctor before you begin your training programme;
- find a local running club, and join it; the members will provide motivation, companionship, advice and support through the long months of training;
- tell your family, friends and colleagues what you are doing; that will help to keep you motivated when it gets tough.

It takes at least nine months of training to work up to a good marathon performance. If you are already running reasonable mileage, you may be able to cut this down to four or five months – but no less.

The training base

Building a solid base of aerobic running is more important for this distance than for any other. You should be running between 25 and 45 miles a week, every week, for at least eight weeks before you begin your specific marathon training. An indication of the necessary mileages is set out in table 12.1:

Table 12.1 Base mileages

Race distance	Beginner	Intermediate	Advanced
Base weekly distance	25–30	30–40	30–45
Max. weekly distance	30–40	40–50	40–60

The training base is the essential foundation of a marathon training programme. If you begin your programme without a solid aerobic base, you are likely to find later in your training that you cannot sustain the mileage and quality that you need. Injury or illness may well constrain your progress, with the result that you lose weeks in the run-up to the marathon.

During your base training period, you should stick to regular aerobic running, with threshold runs to improve your VO_2 max. You can include hills to maintain and improve strength, but you don't need to include speed work at this stage.

The long run

The long run is the lynchpin of the marathon training programme. Depending on your approach, it can be the high spot of your weekly programme, or a dreaded, weekend-busting albatross.

There just isn't a way to train for a marathon without doing a long run, pretty much every week. The long run builds endurance and aerobic capacity, and helps you to develop metabolic pathways to use fat to provide energy. The miles invested in your long runs will be what prevent you from hitting the wall, and enable you to keep going in the brutal last six miles of the race.

How far should your long run be? There is no correct answer to this. Some experts say that 18 miles is long enough; others go up to 22 or 23 miles. If you want to get round the marathon reasonably comfortably, you certainly need to have run 18 miles in training at least once.

How many long runs should you do? You should be doing a long run every weekend (or at least, seven out of eight weekends) during the 16 weeks before the marathon. But they should not all be 20-milers. You can do 16–18 miles most weeks, stepping up to 20 miles perhaps only two or three times before the marathon. You need to get sufficient mileage in your legs, but without tiring yourself out too much. Table 12.2 sets out some guidelines.

Finally, **how fast** should your long run be? Again, this is controversial. Most

Table 12.2 Long run distances[52] and number

Race distance	Beginner	Intermediate	Advanced
Maximum	18–20	20	20–22
Number of peak distance runs	1–2	2–3	3–4

experts agree that the long run should be significantly slower than your target race pace – about 20 per cent slower in most cases.

This will feel awfully slow to many of you. The reason for running as slowly as this is that this will train your fat-burning metabolic pathways, improve your muscles' ability to burn oxygen and store fuel, and increase your endurance.

There are some coaches who believe that long slow distance runs are too slow (Sebastian Coe once famously remarked, 'I've always felt that long, slow distance produces long, slow runners'). But the danger of going too fast is that you risk overdoing it, and possible injury. You will not achieve the purpose by running faster.

Many marathon runners use **long races** in the build-up to the marathon as a way of doing their long run. The months before the London Marathon witness a flood of long (e.g. 20-mile) races, especially around the south-east of England. Using these as training runs is an excellent plan: they build up excitement and motivation, and help you to practise your race-day logistics. However, you should be careful not to run these too hard. It is all too easy to leave your best running on the roads of your training races, and have no energy left when you get to the marathon. In my view, you should certainly not go faster than your intended marathon pace, even though the distance is shorter. One option is to go at your LSD pace (that is, 20 per cent slower than marathon pace) for, say, three-quarters of the race, and then step up to your marathon pace for the last few miles. This will see you finishing strongly, overtaking plenty of runners on the way, give you practice running at your race pace on tired legs and build your confidence, without tiring you out too much.

Whether or not you choose to take part in races before the marathon, you should use your long runs to test your kit and your strategy for eating and drinking. Make sure you do some of your long runs in the clothes and shoes you plan to wear during the marathon, to ensure that they are comfortable and don't rub. If you are going to wear a rhino costume or a spiderman outfit, make sure you practise running in it so that you know what adaptations you need to make. If you are going to drink sports drink during the race, take a bottle with you on your long run and practise sipping it.

'Enjoy yourself at all times; and save your racing for races'.

Bob Davidson, 70

Quality training

If you don't want to improve your time in the marathon, you don't need to read this section. But for everyone who cares about time, there is no getting away from the need to do some strength and speed work before the marathon.

Speed

Clearly, most of your training miles in the run-up to the marathon are going to be aerobic – your weekly long slow distance run, recovery runs and threshold runs. But if you want to run faster, you have to train faster, and this includes speed work.

During the build-up to the marathon, you should probably do speed work once a week. Some elite athletes do more than this, working on a philosophy of high intensity, low mileage training; but for most beginner and club level runners, once a week is enough. For the marathon, you will usually do longer, slower efforts (say, 1000–3000 m) rather than the flat-out sprints.

Strength

Improving your strength is essential for endurance running. In the final stages of any marathon, most runners feel a burning sensation at the front of their thighs (the *quadriceps* muscles). This is because the muscles are exhausted. Strength training increases the endurance of the muscles, their blood supply and their ability to store energy. It increases the lift-off, which increases your stride length and hence your speed. And having strong legs helps to reduce the risk of injury.

Generally the best way to improve your leg strength is to run on hills, either by doing repetitions up a steep hill, or including a hilly section in your aerobic runs (see chapter 9). You can also increase strength by exercises such as hopping, and by using the leg machines in the gym.

Rest

With high weekly mileage, and a long run every week, your body is under enormous stress, especially during the peak weeks. Remember that it is not during the periods of stress that your body adapts and improves, but in the periods of rest in between. Rest is the most important component of the marathon training programme.

The amount of sleep each person needs varies enormously. Margaret Thatcher famously needed only four hours a night. The average person sleeps between seven and eight hours a night. However much you need, you will need more when you increase your training, sometimes by as much as an extra hour a night. Incidentally, one of the benefits of an active, outdoor lifestyle is that few runners suffer from insomnia – they tend to fall asleep as soon as their heads hit the pillow.

It is a good idea to take one rest day a week, to allow the body to recover. Because many runners race or do long runs over the weekend, they often have Fridays as their rest day. Another option is to rest on Monday, but many runners prefer to start the week with a run, and a gentle run usually speeds recovery more than complete rest. You should also make sure that you take an easy week every fourth week, in which you cut back your mileage, to let your body recover.

Training programmes for the marathon

The following pages suggest a 16-week training programme for beginners, intermediate, and advanced runners (by which I mean those willing to run 50 miles a week or more).

In each case, as explained in chapter 10, the training programme follows a series of phases – beginning with base aerobic running, moving on to strength, then speed, then the taper.

You will need to adapt these tables to suit your own pattern and to fit round other priorities in your life. To help you do so, here are some tips to bear in mind:

- you need an **eight-week endurance running base**, running 75 per cent of your peak weekly mileage per week;
- your **long runs** should be at the heart of your schedule; pencil these in first and plan everything around them;
- **plan your weekly mileage** in advance, including easy weeks; and try to stick to it; don't increase the weekly mileage too fast or you will get injured (see chapter 10);
- pencil in significant events in your life, such as birthdays or travel plans; and include key social events with your partner or family;
- if you **get behind with your schedule** – for example because of injury – don't try to catch up or jump back into the levels of your original schedule; go back to where you left off, and progress from there.

Tapering

In the three weeks before the marathon, you should cut back your running mileage. This is called 'tapering'. Tapering enables your body to rest, rebuild its energy stores and be fully hydrated for the race.

With three weeks to go, cut your weekly mileage to 75 per cent of your peak. With two weeks to go, cut back to 50 per cent. And in the final week, run just 25 per cent of your peak weekly mileage.

It is the training you do months before the race that will determine your success. In the days before the race you can make yourself tired and run down your energy levels, but there is no time for the cycle of stress and adaptation to occur to improve your performance.

Although you are cutting the distances you run, you should not cut back the **intensity** of your training until the final week. For example, you should continue to do track work, at or about your race pace, but cut the number of repetitions.

Don't fall into the trap of doing too much **cross training** in these final weeks. Many athletes get restless because of the lack of activity, and start to swim and cycle. Far from storing up energy, this can result in higher energy expenditure than if you were to keep on running. Reserve your enthusiasm for swimming for after the marathon.

For the final few days before the race, cut your running back to nothing. The key is to get plenty of rest. The day before the race you may want to do a few strides to keep the blood flowing, and stretch, but you should not run.

Runners all too frequently come down with an infection during the tapering phase before a marathon. See chapter 8 for advice on how to minimise this risk.

Carbo-loading

Your nutritional needs before and during running are discussed in chapters 6 and 7. For marathons, you should spend the last three to six days before the race increasing your intake of both carbohydrates and water, to ensure that your muscle glycogen is fully stocked, and that you are fully hydrated for the race. Don't just eat pasta: make sure you eat plenty of fruit, vegetables and grains. There are some ideas in chapter 7.

The old practice of **carbo-depleting** just before the carbo-loading phase has now fallen out of favour, as there is no evidence that it works.

The day before the marathon

Your main goal the day before the marathon is to rest as much as you can. On marathon day, you need to expend about twice your normal daily energy output, which means you want your fuel stores fully stocked.

Many of the big city marathons have 'expos' for a few days before the marathon, to which you have to go to pick up your running number and t-shirt. These are generally a great way to get in the mood, and if you like shopping for running gear, good places to browse for bargains in the stalls.

If your marathon is not in your home town, you should try to arrive at least two days before the race, so that you can relax during the day, and don't spend it travelling, or having to hurry round the marathon expo.

> 'Running big city marathons is a great way to visit other cities. Take a few days to relax and sight-see while you are there.'
>
> *George Tarbuck*

You should not run the day before the marathon. You can, if you wish, do some gentle strides to maintain flexibility and keep your legs mobile, but be careful not to overdo it.

During the day before the marathon, you should be drinking plenty of water (keep a water bottle in your hand all day) and avoiding diuretics such as tea, coffee and alcohol. One good idea is to drink diluted carbohydrate drinks, so that you are also carbo-loading as you drink. Eat plenty of carbohydrates, and avoid foods that might upset your stomach.

One way to get a lot of support in a marathon is to have your name stencilled onto your t-shirt. You can get this done in shops that sell football shirts, which have equipment to print the players' names on sports shirts. You'll be amazed at how much of a lift it gives you when the crowd calls out your name during the race.

The night before the marathon, lay out all your kit for the next day. Pin your number on your t-shirt, and ensure that you have everything you need ready to take with you. (Use the packing checklist in chapter 11.) In many big city marathons, you are required to use the kitbag provided for you at the expo – so don't try to use your own bag if this is the case.

Race day

Ideally, you should have a big **breakfast**, about three hours before the race begins. Some people can manage a smaller gap between breakfast and the race, some need longer: you will have found out from your training runs what works for you. Race day breakfast should be easily digested carbohydrates. I have a tradition of eating a honey and banana sandwich, but porridge, cereal or bagels would be fine. Avoid fried foods, unless you have tried this in training.

Get to the start in good time, so that you have time to go to the toilet and hand in your kitbag. You don't want to be stressed because you are short of time. If it is cold, remember to wear a bin-liner after you have handed in your kit to keep you warm and dry before the start. The conventional advice is that you should stop drinking about two hours before the race. Some runners keep sipping water right up to the start; my experience is that this makes me need to urinate during the first mile of the race.

I don't warm up before the marathon – I think the race is long enough already. Your main objective at this stage is to conserve your glycogen stores. Instead, I prefer to start off slowly and warm up during the first couple of miles. If you do want to warm up a little, jog for half a mile, and don't do any high intensity running that will be fuelled by glycogen.

At the start, line up with the people who are running at your pace. There are usually markers along the side of the start, or sometimes separate pens, which show where you should start off depending on your likely completion time. Don't start further up the field than is right for you: you will be swept off too fast, which will wreck your chances of meeting your goal; and it is annoying and dangerous for faster runners to have to weave around you in the first mile of the race.

Your enjoyment of the marathon, and your performance, will be decided in the first five miles. Inexperienced marathon runners almost all shoot off too fast. You have rested, so you feel strong; the adrenalin is pumping; and the crowds are urging you on. The pace feels ridiculously slow compared to all the running you have done in training. All the runners around you have set off faster than you. At this point, your mind can play tricks on you. You can convince yourself that you could sustain this pace for 26.2 miles, and finish much faster than anyone, including you, expected. All this is rubbish: don't be one of the lemmings.

Start the race 10–20 seconds a mile **slower** than your target race pace. You can easily make this up later – after all, you have a long way to go! Running slowly can be very difficult to do, because the runners around you will sweep you along faster. But remind yourself that every 10 seconds a mile too fast in the first few miles will cost you a minute a mile in the final six miles. Instead, chat to other runners, enjoy the sights and the crowd, and smile at the supporters.

> 'Nothing is more certain than the defeat of the man who gives up.'
>
> *George Sheehan*

If you find at the first mile marker that you have set off too fast: **stop and walk**. This is about the only way of giving yourself a chance to recover, and breaking your rhythm. (The day I first ran under 40 minutes for 10 km, I ran the first kilometre in 3:06 – which was far too fast. I walked the first half of the second kilometre to get myself back on schedule.)

During the early miles of a big marathon, the route is often crowded, before the runners begin to spread out. Resist the temptation to weave around slower runners. This uses up energy, and is stressful. Fall in behind them until you can pass them easily. It won't do you any harm to slow down a bit: you are probably going too fast anyway.

When I am running a marathon, I divide it mentally into three parts: the first half marathon, a hard seven miles, and the gruelling last six miles.

For the first half of the marathon, your mission is to keep relaxed, conserve energy and find your rhythm. You should be feeling very strong, and having to fight the urge to go faster. Start drinking a little at every water station, even if you don't feel thirsty yet.

Assess your position at half way. Ideally, you will have used up 49–51 per cent of your target marathon time. You should feel fresh and strong. If you are working hard to maintain this pace, or if you are breathing heavily, then you are running too fast, and may need to adjust your goal for this marathon.

The next seven miles are mentally tough. Concentrate on staying relaxed, keep your head up and your shoulders back, and think about your running form. This is where many runners begin to slow down without realising it. Don't rely on the runners around you to maintain your pace: they are probably slowing down. Keep an

eye on your watch as you pass the mile markers. If you feel you are beginning to tire, it is often a good idea to *speed up* a little – a change of pace reinvigorates your legs, and gives you a mental boost. Take your sports drink or gels, and promise them to yourself as rewards for getting to the next milestone or drinks station.

It is often said that the halfway stage of a marathon is 20 miles; and it is certainly true that the last six miles are always as hard, mentally and physically, as the first twenty. They are also always harder than you think they are going to be. There is no suitable preparation for the experience. The battle is mainly in your mind. As you run the last six miles, remind yourself that you have done the training (you *have* done the training, haven't you?) and that you have earned the right to achieve your goal. Think of all those early winter mornings, running in the cold and rain; think of those weekend long runs; those gut-wrenching track sessions. Remind yourself that, when the race has finished, the pain and nausea will go away rapidly; and that if you keep running you will get there more quickly. Visualise success, and imagine what your friends and family will say when you are finished. Imagine the photograph of you crossing the finish line.

I have a personal trick that works for me. Smile. However much effort I am putting in, I find that if I force myself to smile, I get an extra spring in my step.

After the marathon

Congratulations! You are entitled to be very proud of what you have achieved.

Immediately after you finish, your priority should be to keep moving. Pick up your kitbag, change into dry clothes, and put on your medal proudly. But don't whatever you do sit down, or you risk heatstroke and muscle cramps.

You should force yourself to drink. Dilute sports drinks are best, so that you are getting carbohydrates as well, which aid fluid absorption. Keep drinking even if you feel nauseous. Have a look at the guidelines in chapter 7.

Your aim should be to get carbohydrates inside you within half an hour. This can be a cheese sandwich, sports drink, bagel, or anything else you fancy. You probably won't be hungry, but it is essential to refuel as fast as you can to help your muscles repair. Fruit – particularly a banana – is very good.

Some athletes have cold showers or ice baths after a race, to reduce the bruising within their muscles. I have always regarded this as too brutal, but I suspect that it helps them to recover more quickly.

After about twenty minutes of walking, you will probably want to sit or lie down. At this point, listen to your body and rest.

How quickly should you return to running after a marathon? Again, listen to your body. Most runners take at least a week off running altogether, and then come back to running gradually after that. I like to cycle during the week after a marathon, as this seems to increase the blood flow and help stiff muscles to recover. Most experts advise that you should take at least four days off.

You can spend the time deciding where you are going to run your next marathon . . .

Running for Fitness

Training schedules for the marathon

Table 12.1 Sample training schedule for marathon: beginner

Weeks	Phase	Miles	Mon	Tue	Wed	Thu	Fri	Sat	Sun
Base	Base	25		6 easy	3 thresh	3 thresh		6 easy	10 slow
16	Base	27		3 fartlek	6 easy	3 thresh		3 easy	12 slow
15	Base	29		6 easy	4 easy	4 thresh		3 easy	12 slow
14	Base	29		6 easy	4 easy	4 thresh		3 easy	12 slow
13	Strength E	22		2 hills	4 easy	4 fartlek		3 easy	9 slow
12	Strength	31		4 hills	6 easy	4 thresh		5 easy	12 slow
11	Strength	34		3 hills	6 easy	4 thresh		3 easy	18 slow
10	Strength	34		3 hills	6 easy	4 fartlek		5 easy	16 slow
9	Speed E	26		4 easy	5 easy	3 interval		1 stride	13 race
8	Speed	35		4 fartlek	6 easy	4 interval		5 easy	16 slow
7	Speed	34		4 thresh	4 easy	3 interval		3 easy	20 slow
6	Speed	35		4 fartlek	6 easy	4 interval		5 easy	16 slow
5	Speed E	28		3 thresh	6 easy	4 interval		3 easy	12 slow
4	Peak	35		4 fartlek	6 easy	2 interval		3 easy	20 slow
3	Taper	25		3 thresh	6 easy	1 interval		3 easy	12 slow
2	Taper	18		2 fartlek	4 easy	1 interval		3 easy	8 slow
1	Taper	8 + race		3 strides	3 easy	2 easy			26.2 race

Sample interval sessions:

Wk 9   12 × 400 m at 5 km pace; 45 sec recovery
Wk 8   2 sets of 3 × 1000 m at 3 km pace; 120 sec recovery; 1 lap jog between sets
Wk 7   3 sets of 4 × 400 m at 800 m pace; 150 sec recovery; 1 lap jog between sets
Wk 6   400 m, 600 m, 800 m, 1200 m, 1600 m, 1200 m, 800 m, 600 m, 400 m (+5 sec/lap as +distance); 60 sec recovery
Wk 5   4 × 1600 m at 5 km pace; 90 sec recovery
Wk 4   6 × 600 m at 1500 m pace; 120 sec recovery
Wk 3   5 × 400 m at 3 km pace; 45 sec recovery
Wk 2   10 × 200 m at 400 m pace; 180 sec recovery

Table 12.2 Sample training schedule for marathon: intermediate

Weeks	Phase	Miles	Mon	Tue	Wed	Thu	Fri	Sat	Sun
Base	Base	30		5 easy	3 thresh	5 easy		5 easy	12 slow
16	Base	33		4 fartlek	6 easy	4 thresh		5 easy	14 slow
15	Base	35	5 easy	4 fartlek	4 easy	3 thresh		5 easy	14 slow
14	Base	37	5 easy	4 fartlek	5 easy	4 thresh		5 easy	14 slow
13	Strength E	28	5 easy	2 hills	4 easy	4 fartlek		5 easy	8 slow
12	Strength	40	6 easy	4 hills	6 easy	4 thresh		6 easy	14 slow
11	Strength	43	6 easy	3 hills	6 easy	4 thresh		6 easy	18 slow
10	Strength	44	6 easy	4 hills	6 easy	4 fartlek		4 easy	20 slow
9	Speed E	31	3 fartlek	8 practice	3 easy	3 interval		1 stride	13 race
8	Speed	44	3 easy	9 practice	4 easy	4 interval		6 easy	18 slow
7	Speed	41	3 easy	10 practice	4 easy	3 interval		1 stride	20 slow
6	Speed	44	3 easy	11 practice	4 easy	4 interval		6 easy	16 slow
5	Speed E	29	3 easy	12 practice	3 easy	4 interval		3 easy	12 slow
4	Peak	44	3 easy	4 thresh	3 easy	2 interval		4 easy	20 slow
3	Taper	31	4 easy	5 easy	5 easy	1 interval		4 easy	12 slow
2	Taper	22	4 easy	2 fartlek	4 easy	1 interval		3 easy	8 slow
1	Taper	11 + race		4 easy	4 easy	3 strides			26.2 race

Sample interval sessions:

Wk 9 12 × 400 m at 5 km pace; 45 sec recovery

Wk 8 2 sets of 3 × 1000 m at 3 km pace; 120 sec recovery; 1 lap jog between sets

Wk 7 3 sets of 4 × 400 m at 800 m pace; 150 sec recovery; 1 lap jog between sets

Wk 6 400 m, 600 m, 800 m, 1200 m, 1600 m, 1200 m, 800 m, 600 m, 400 m (+5 sec/lap as +distance); 60 sec recovery

Wk 5 4 × 1600 m at 5 km pace; 90 sec recovery

Wk 4 6 × 600 m at 1500 m pace; 120 sec recovery

Wk 3 5 × 400 m at 3 km pace; 45 sec recovery

Wk 2 10 × 200 m at 400 m pace; 180 sec recovery

Table 12.3 Sample training schedule for marathon: advanced

Weeks	Phase	Miles	Mon	Tue	Wed	Thu	Fri	Sat	Sun
Base	Base	35	5 easy	4 fartlek	5 easy	4 thresh		5 easy	12 slow
16	Base	38	5 easy	4 fartlek	6 easy	4 thresh		5 easy	14 slow
15	Base	40	6 easy	4 fartlek	6 easy	3 thresh		5 easy	16 slow
14	Base	42	6 easy	4 fartlek	6 easy	4 thresh		6 easy	16 slow
13	Strength E	32	4 easy	4 fartlek	4 easy	2 hills		6 easy	12 slow
12	Strength	44	6 easy	8 practice	6 easy	4 hills		6 easy	14 slow
11	Strength	46	5 easy	10 practice	5 easy	3 hills		6 easy	16 slow
10	Strength	50	5 easy	12 practice	6 easy	4 hills		3 easy	20 slow
9	Speed E	31	3 easy	8 practice	3 easy	3 interval		1 stride	13 race
8	Speed	45	3 easy	13 practice	4 easy	4 interval		3 easy	18 slow
7	Speed	48	4 easy	14 practice	4 easy	3 interval		3 easy	20 slow
6	Speed	49	4 easy	15 practice	4 easy	4 interval		6 easy	16 slow
5	Speed E	33	3 easy	8 practice	3 easy	4 interval		3 easy	12 slow
4	Peak	50	4 easy	16 practice	4 easy	2 interval		4 easy	20 slow
3	Taper	35	5 easy	5 thresh	6 easy	1 interval		6 easy	12 slow
2	Taper	25	5 easy	3 fartlek	4 easy	1 interval		4 easy	8 slow
1	Taper	12 + race		5 easy	4 easy	3 strides			26.2 race

Sample interval sessions:

Wk 9 12×400 m at 5 km pace; 45 sec recovery
Wk 8 2 sets of 3×1000 m at 3 km pace; 120 sec recovery; 1 lap jog between sets
Wk 7 3 sets of 4×400 m at 800 m pace; 150 sec recovery; 1 lap jog between sets
Wk 6 400 m, 600 m, 800 m, 1200 m, 1600 m, 1200 m, 800 m, 600 m, 400 m (+5 sec/lap as +distance); 60 sec recovery
Wk 5 4×1600 m at 5 km pace; 90 sec recovery
Wk 4 6×600 m at 1500 m pace; 120 sec recovery
Wk 3 5×400 m at 3 km pace; 45 sec recovery
Wk 2 10×200 m at 400 m pace; 180 sec recovery

13 Further reading

This chapter is an annotated reading list for people who want to know more about running. This is not intended to be an exhaustive list – there are far too many books and articles for that. It simply highlights the most important books, and some personal favourites. The books are listed in alphabetical order by author.

Anita Bean, *The Complete Guide to Sports Nutrition* (2000)
Anita Bean is a former body-builder, whose book is comprehensive and easy to read. It is packed with examples (including menu plans) to bring the theories to life. Bean is not afraid to roll up her sleeves and she gets stuck into the biochemistry, but everything is presented in an approachable way.

Jack Daniels, *Daniels' Running Formula* (1998)
Jack Daniels's book is a must-have classic that should appear on the bookshelf of every serious runner with a scientific bent. Daniels's approach is to divide training into five quite precise zones, based on the runner's VO_2 max. All training should happen in one of those zones (and by implication, any running outside one of these zones is junk miles). Daniels also proposes a complex programme of periodization of training to obtain the best benefits. The book is based on a great deal of scientific research, and is quite numerical.

Jeff Galloway, *Galloway's Book on Running* (1984)
The top-selling book in the world on running, this is a standard text. In the current version it covers training for the 5 km, 10 km and half marathon (if you want to know about marathons you'll have to buy a separate book, *Marathon: you can do it!*). Galloway's approach can occasionally seem a little old-fashioned, but there is a lot of good sense in this book.

Bob Glover and Shelly-lynn Florence Glover, *The Competitive Runner's Handbook* (1983)
A comprehensive book tightly packed with useful information for runners who want to race. The Glovers are leading lights in the New York Road Runner's Club, and Bob Glover has thirty years' experience of coaching. A book to dip into, rather than read in a single sitting.

Hal Higdon, *Marathon: The Ultimate Training Guide* (1999)

Hal Higdon is a runner and writer, contributing a popular column for *Runner's World* magazine. He also organises training camps in the US for runners who want to run a marathon. His book on the marathon is a classic, that has inspired thousands of people to take to the roads. Simple and well-written, in a chatty style, it draws on his deep reservoirs of knowledge and experience. Higdon has written more than thirty other books, including *Smart Running*, which contains lots of useful material, but in a slightly irritating question and answer format.

Frank Horwill, *An Obsession for Running* (1991)

Horwill's slim volume describes his own odyssey, including his fight with stomach cancer, while explaining the theory behind his five-pace training theory. More than anyone else, Horwill was the drive behind the renaissance of English middle distance running in the 1970s and 1980s. Peter Coe (Sebastian Coe's father and coach) credits Horwill with the breakthroughs in training on which Coe's remarkable career was built.

Tim Noakes, *The Lore of Running* (2001)

This is the ultimate runner's reference book. Tim Noakes is a marathon runner, and Professor of Sports Science at the University of Cape Town. Noakes covers each issue comprehensively, setting out the evidence and then proposing his own conclusions (but always distinguishing his own comments from the facts). The latest edition (currently only available in hardback, and weighing in at over 1200 pages) was published in 2001, and has been significantly revised.

Pete Pfitzinger and Scott Douglas, *Road Racing for Serious Runners* (1999)

This is an excellent practical manual for training for races from 5 km to the marathon. The book assumes a reasonably high starting point, both in terms of running ability and knowledge about the subject. The approach owes much to the techniques of Jack Daniels, and the book sets out simple and specific training programmes. It is clearly and simply written. Unusually (and unexpectedly, given the title) there is advice on training for cross-country.

George Sheehan, *Running to Win* (1992); *Personal Best* (1989); *Running and Being* (1978)

George Sheehan was a medical doctor who took up running in his mid-forties. Five years later he set a world record for the mile for a 50-year-old (4:47). He ran more than 60 marathons, including a personal best of 3:01 at the age of 61. In 1968 he began to write about running for a local newspaper; ten years later his book *Running and Being* became a national bestseller. He established himself as the foremost philosopher of running, with a knack for expressing in words the ideas that many runners have subconsciously about their running. Sheehan's books are an absolute inspiration for every runner. He died in 1993.

14 Resources

Websites

Amateur Athletics Association
http://www.englandathletics.org.uk/

Athletic Association of Wales
http://www.welshathletics.org/

Athletics Weekly
http://www.athletics-weekly.co.uk/

British Milers Club
http://www.britishmilersclub.com/

British Triathlon Association
http://www.britishtriathlon.co.uk/

British Veterans Athletic Federation
http://www.bvaf.org.uk/

Central Council of Physical Recreation
http://www.ccpr.org.uk/

Directory of UK Podiatrists
http://www.podiatrypages.co.uk/

Hal Higdon's Marathon Training
http://www.halhigdon.com/

Less Bounce Sports Bras
http://www.lessbounce.com/

Northern Ireland Athletic Federation
http://www.niathletics.org/

Peak Performance Online
http://www.pponline.co.uk/

Run the Planet
http://www.runtheplanet.com/

Runner's World
http://www.runnersworld.co.uk/

Runner's World Women's Running
http://www.womens-running.com/

Scottish Athletics
http://www.saf.org.uk/

Serpentine Running Club
http://www.serpentine.org.uk/

Sports Aid
http://www.sportsaid.org.uk/

Sports Coach
http://www.brianmac.demon.co.uk/

Sports Injury Clinic
http://www.sportsinjuryclinic.net/

Tales of the Penguin (John Bingham)
http://www.waddleon.com/

The London Marathon
http://www.london-marathon.co.uk/

UK Athletics
http://www.ukathletics.net/

UK Athletics Club Directory
http://www.runtrackdir.com/ukclubs

UK Results
http://www.ukresults.net/

UK Running Track Directory
http://www.runtrackdir.com/

UK Sport
http://www.uksport.gov.uk/

World Association of Veteran Athletes
http://www.wava.org/

By post

UK Athletics, Athletics House,
10 Harborne Road, Edgbaston,
Birmingham, B15 3AA.
Tel: 0121 456 5098; Fax: 0121 456 8752

15 References

1 George Sheehan, *Running to Win* (Rodale Press, 1992).

2 American Heart Association, *Exercise (Physical Activity) Scientific Position* (1999). http://www.justmove.org/myfitness/lowarticles/lowframes.cfm?Target=exercise.html

3 See, for example, Health Development Agency, *Health Promotion Effectiveness Reviews, Summary Bulletin 14* (1998).

4 Tim Noakes, *The Lore of Running* (Oxford University Press, 2001).

5 See, for example, Ralph Paffenbarger's analysis of 17,000 Harvard University alumni in R. S. Paffenbarger, Jr. and I. M. Lee, *Physical Activity and Fitness for Health and Longevity* (Res Q Exerc Sport, 1996).

6 Tim Noakes, *The Lore of Running* (Oxford University Press, 2001), pp. 1125.

7 National Audit Office, *Obesity in England*, Office of the Comptroller and Auditor General, February 2001.

8 Report of a WHO Consultation on Obesity, 3–5 June 1997, Geneva, WHO/NUT/NCD/98.1.

9 For a summary of these, see Tim Noakes, *The Lore of Running* (Oxford University Press, 2001), pp. 718–23.

10 Ibid.

11 Ibid., p. 423.

12 See http://www.serpentine.org.uk/routes/.

13 See http://www.accuroute.co.uk/.

14 http://www.pegasussoftware.com/.

15 http://www.science-sportsware.dk/.

16 Ethylene Vinyl Acetate.

17 www.fitsense.com.

18 A. E. Atwater, 'Gender differences in distance running', in P. R. Cavanagh (ed.), *Biomechanics of Distance Running* (Human Kinetics, 1990), pp. 321–62.

19 E. M. Hennig, 'Gender difference for running in athletic footwear', *Proceedings of the 5th Symposium on Footwear Biomechanics* (ed. Hennig and Stacoff), 2001.

20 L. Speroff and D. B. Redwine (1980) 'Exercise and menstrual function', *Physician and Sportsmedicine 8* (May), pp. 42–52. Also J. M. Lutter and S. Cishman (1982) 'Menstrual patterns in female runners', *Physician and Sportsmedicine 10* (September), pp. 60–72.

21 Dagny Scott, *The Complete Book of Women's Running* (Rodale Press, 2000).

22 'Adolescent Girls: Factors Influencing Low and High Body Image', *Melpomene* (1995), 14(2): 14–22.

23 Report of the US Surgeon General, *Physical Activity and Health* (1996).

24 For example, Anita Bean, *The Complete Guide to Sports Nutrition* (A&C Black, 2000).

25 C. Williams and J. T. Devlin (eds), *Food, Nutrition and Performance: An International Scientific Consensus* (Chapman & Hall, 1992).

26 This section owes much to Anita Bean, *The Complete Guide to Sports Nutrition* (A&C Black, 2000).

27 M. H. Williams, *Nutrition for Health, Fitness and Sport* (McGraw-Hill, 1999).

28 Anita Bean, *The Complete Guide to Sports Nutrition* (A&C Black, 2000), p. 113.

29 British Nutrition Foundation, see http://www.nutrition.org.uk/.

30 J. L. Fallowfield, C. Williams, J. Booth, B. H. Choo, and S. Growns, 'Effect of water ingestion on endurance capacity during prolonged running', *Journal of Sports Sciences*, 14, (April 1996), pp. 497–502.

31 National Athletic Trainers' Association Position Statement: Fluid Replacement for Athletes, *Journal of Athletic Training* (2000), 35(2): 212–24. See http://www.nata.org/.

32 T. D. Noakes, N. Goodwin, B. L. Rayner, T. Brankin, and R. K. N. Taylor (1985) 'Water intoxication: a possible complication of endurance exercise', *Medicine and Science in Sports and Exercise*, 17: 370–5.

33 Tim Noakes, *The Lore of Running* (Oxford University Press, 2001), pp. 265–73.

34 Reproduced at: http://sportsmedicine.about.com/library/bl_acsm_fluid.htm.

35 Hal Higdon, *Marathon: The Ultimate Training Guide* (Rodale Press, 1999).

36 S. M. Shirreffs *et al.* (1996), 'Post exercise rehydration in man: effects of volume consumed and drink sodium content', *Med. Sci. Sport Ex.*, 28.

37 Tim Noakes, *The Lore of Running* (Oxford University Press, 2001), p. 835.

38 A. R. Coggan and E. F. Coyle, 'Carbohydrate ingestion during prolonged exercise: effects on metabolism and performance', in J. Holloszy (ed.), *Exercise and Sports Science Reviews*, vol. 19 (Williams & Wilkins, 1991), pp. 1–40.

39 M. L. Gross, K. B. Davlin, and P. M. Evanski, 'Effectiveness of orthotic shoe inserts in the long distance runner', *American Journal of Sports Medicine*, 19 (1991), 409–12.

40 P. G. Hanson and D. K. Flaherty, Immunological responses to training in conditioned runners, *Clinical Sciences*, 60 (1981), 225–8.

41 D. C. Nieman, L. M. Johanssen, J. W. Lee, and K. Arabatzis, 'Infectious Episodes in Runners Before and After the Los Angeles Marathon', *Journal of Sports Medicine and Physical Fitness*, 30 (1990), 316–28.

42 Tim Noakes, *The Lore of Running* (Oxford University Press, 2001).

43 Tim Noakes, *The Lore of Running* (Oxford University Press, 2001).

44 Frank Horwill, *An Obsession for Running* (British Milers' Club, 1991).

45 http://www.serpentine.org.uk/advice/coach/.

46 Tim Noakes, *The Lore of Running* (Oxford University Press, 2001).

47 Jack Daniels, *Daniels' Running Formula* (Human Kinetics, 1998).

48 Jack Daniels, *Daniels' Running Formula* (Human Kinetics, 1998).

49 Adapted from Bob Glover and Shelly-lynn Florence Glover, *The Competitive Runners Handbook*, second edition (Penguin, 1999).

50 Adapted from Bob Glover and Shelly-lynn Florence Glover, *The Competitive Runners Handbook*, second edition (Penguin, 1999).

51 Hal Higdon, *Marathon: The Ultimate Training Guide* (Rodale Press, 1999).

52 Adapted from Bob Glover and Shelly-lynn Florence Glover, *The Competitive Runners Handbook*, second edition (Penguin, 1999).

Index

Note: page references in **bold** refer to illustrations and figures.